LEAD
FROM THE
HEART™

LEAD
FROM THE
HEART™

TRANSFORMATIONAL LEADERSHIP FOR THE 21ST CENTURY

MARK C. CROWLEY

BALBOA.
PRESS

A DIVISION OF HAY HOUSE

Balboa Press books may be ordered through booksellers or by contacting:

Balboa Press
A Division of Hay House
1663 Liberty Drive
Bloomington, IN 47403
www.balboapress.com
1-(877) 407-4847

Because of the dynamic nature of the Internet, any web addresses or links contained in this book may have changed since publication and may no longer be valid. The views expressed in this work are solely those of the author and do not necessarily reflect the views of the publisher, and the publisher hereby disclaims any responsibility for them.

Cover artwork designed by Morgan Ervin

ISBN: 978-1-4525-3541-8 (e)
ISBN: 978-1-4525-3540-1 (sc)
ISBN: 978-1-4525-3542-5 (hc)

Library of Congress Control Number: 2011908405

Printed in the United States of America

Balboa Press rev. date: 7/5/2011

For my wife, Carol, who never wavered in her belief that I was on purpose in writing this book and who, more than anyone, gave me the heart to complete it.

CONTENTS

INTRODUCTION

Every human heart is human.
Henry Wadsworth Longfellow

I was raised by wolves.

There's no literal truth to this statement and yet it feels totally accurate as an explanation for the inhuman and often heartless form of care I received during most of my childhood. Ironically, wolves have quite a good reputation for rearing their young; had I really been left to their care, I'm inclined to believe their nurturing instincts would have been far superior to those of the humans who did raise me. They would almost have to be.

One of my brothers is certain my father's intention was to *destroy* the lives of all his children. While I've never wanted to accept this assertion as truth - who wants to believe that of their own father? - the psychic wounds we all suffered were too numerous, deep and enduring to argue otherwise.

My father was a man who virtually never conveyed his love or esteem for me. Instead, for reasons I'll never fully understand, starting when I was very little, he went to work on dismantling my sense of well being. Some inner directive made him overtly destructive, and rarely constructive, in his approach to motivating my behavior and achievement.

He was an extremely volatile person who came home from work almost every night enraged. Although I sincerely tried, nothing I did could ever please him. This was dispiriting to me as a young boy, of course, but how he chose to express his displeasure did the most harm. He would scream. The reverberation of his yelling undoubtedly did cellular damage to me, but even more injurious were the things he said – things he wanted me to believe about myself and to know he believed about me. Using ten dollar words of piercing pain and hurt, my father took direct hits on my equilibrium and self-confidence.

To convey his belief that I lacked ambition, he called me *shiftless*. He told me I was *mendacious* (a liar), an *ingrate* (ungrateful) and had *no milk of human kindness* (no concern or regard for others). He characterized me as being *pusillanimous* (one of the most destructive words in our language) meaning he saw me as having a contemptible lack of boldness and resolve. In those days, there was no Google search engine – no convenient way of finding all of the "words which destroy children's spirits." He had to make a more concerted effort. I didn't even know the meaning of his expressions when I first heard them – but the venomous intonation he used to express them conveyed their inherent meaning.

He used the Latin phrase, *Non compos mentis*, to assert that I had an inferior mind but relied upon the King's English to more accessibly communicate his lack of confidence in me. Repeatedly, for years upon years, he forecasted that mine would be a life of failure telling me I would never *measure up* and that I wouldn't *ever amount to anything in life*. He instilled in me that I lacked. I learned from him that whatever I did, whoever I would become, in his eyes, I would never be enough.

While it's a mystery to me why I was born to be parented by someone so dysfunctional and abusive, it's equally curious that a safe haven – an alternative universe – was placed in the house right next door. When I was nine-years-old, my mother died and my father quickly remarried. My new step-mother was entirely indifferent and unwelcoming to me and insisted I spend little time at home. I was effectively forced to find some place else to go after school each day.

I chose to go next door because my two best friends lived there. It didn't seem to matter to their mother that, all of a sudden, I was coming over *every* day and staying until very late. Knowing I had almost nowhere else to go, this greatly heartened me. But a form of spiritual fireworks exploded inside me when my friends' mother told me directly that I was not only welcome in her home but that she *wanted* me there. Soon, she was laughing at my jokes, taking an interest in my school work, and soliciting my observations about the world. More than anything, she validated what I wanted to believe was my real truth – that I was a great kid with wonderful potential. Her generous, thoughtful and consistent gestures of care, encouragement and validation sustained me over many years and made an enormous difference to my surviving such an insane ordeal.

When I turned eighteen, my father kicked me out of the house. Even with all of the disharmony in our home, his decision caught me by complete surprise. It had never crossed my mind that he wouldn't support me while I attended college. But he didn't. While quite wealthy, he offered no financial assistance. He provided no direction or guidance. I moved into an apartment and into five of the most difficult and stressful years of my life. Not once did he check in to see if I was holding up. I found new friends who routinely assured me I would endure and succeed. They empathized with what I was going through and found ways to show their care. Part of my motivation to get through college was to prove to myself that my father had been wrong about me. That's a corrupt motivation, of course, and one driven by fear and feelings of unworthiness. But my succeeding had much more to do with the professors, bosses and other people in my life who saw my potential and made impactful gestures of care at just the right moments to support my progress. What an enormous difference those things made in my life.

It's been over thirty years since the end of my childhood and it's taken a long part of that time for me to make complete peace with all I endured growing up. But in the end, I came to more than just accept and forgive all that occurred. I came to believe it all happened for a reason – for a *purpose.*

I sincerely believe I had the childhood experiences I did for the purpose of discovering a more productive and sustainable way of relating to and leading people, a new and transformational model that inspires people to perform and contribute to their highest potential all the while ensuring *all* constituencies – employers, shareholders and workers – routinely flourish.

Much like children in the Great Depression whose early deprivation influenced them to scrimp and save for the rest of their lives, my severe upbringing changed my original wiring. It made me infinitely more sensitive to people and gave me unusual insight into what people needed to thrive. All the abuse and fundamental lack of support led me to treat people I was supervising more humanely and to find ways of maximizing their talents. All the years I was growing up, I used to fantasize about how much more of my potential could have been realized had I been better cared for and more thoughtfully directed. Knowing all the things I felt I had missed out on – and always had wanted – I made the decision to give those things to others.

Essentially, this had to do with:

- Genuinely and openly valuing people as individuals.

- Fostering a sense of well being in them so they could perform at high levels.

- Identifying their raw talents and dreaming how much more they could become with additional development and coaching.

- Expressing my deep belief in them – reinforcing their self-confidence.

- Finding ways to share skills and information I already had mastered to accelerate their effectiveness.

- Encouraging them when a task was challenging or when I sensed their fear, apprehension, or doubt about their ability to achieve.

- Making a deliberate point of honoring and recognizing achievements – but also acknowledging personal initiative, professional growth, and progress made toward attaining goals.

What I chose to do is really basic and fundamental – but quite uncommon in business. As a hard-charging business leader, and a man, I nurtured and supported the human needs in people so they could perform to their greatest potential. I did all this unconsciously at first and all my teams excelled. For many years, I took the success for granted and didn't really connect the dots. But after several years had passed and I had the experience of leading myriad business units and teams of people, it became quite evident that the leadership practices I had implemented in response to a profoundly painful childhood were influencing people to be remarkably engaged and high achieving. It didn't matter what kind of childhood anyone had or what role people were performing; the effects were identical. I discovered that people never outgrow the need for the kind of care I was providing. And while we expect people to be complete by the time they join the workforce, the truth is no one is ever fully developed or self-assured. Moreover, I believe *all* people feel limited in some way and can be transformed through thoughtful coaching and encouragement. More than anything, my experience has taught me that people are virtually *unlimited* given the right support.

When I first sat down to write this book, I had a very straightforward ambition: to share four specific leadership practices my experience proved had a powerful effect on people and inspired their highest engagement and productivity. But as I closed myself off and began real consideration into what I would write, I dug deeper into the question of *why* these practices had been so effective on other people. I had always known *that* they worked; but my original motivation for employing them was because I believed they would have worked for *me*.

Inevitably, I came to more fully understand that what I had been doing all along was positively affecting the hearts in people. I realized that people had responded to this kind of leadership because they could feel I was someone who genuinely cared and who made an effort to express that to them. People had used feeling in their hearts to sense that who they were and what they contributed was authentically valued, and these feelings motivated them to perform at extraordinary levels.

My epiphany was that I had brought heart into leadership and this revelation stopped me in my tracks.

The idea of leading with *any* amount of heart flies in the face of our collective belief that the heart acts like kryptonite in business. We associate the heart in the workplace as being soft, sentimental, and antithetical to driving profit. We frown on heart. In the moment, I was greatly conflicted. I knew from my own twenty-five years of leadership experience that people had scaled the tallest mountains for me simply because I recognized their individual genius, helped them to develop it, put it to its best use and helped them to find gratification in the work they did. There was no question in my mind that heart had been the *catalyst* for their exceptional achievement.

At the same time, I knew I had to be a realist. Because our longstanding paradigm and worldview in business is that the heart will only get you into trouble, I understood immediately that my own personal experience could be judged as anecdotal; a book that argues we need to bring the heart into balance with the brain in leadership was at great risk of being summarily rejected.

My inclination wasn't to back away from writing the book, but to instead go in search of research and science that might support my hypothesis. Initially, in seemed like a wild-goose chase, but then I came upon one stunning piece of information after another. I devoted nearly a full year to the effort and, ultimately, was able to prove that we've been long misled. Our cultural beliefs which tell us to not connect to people we supervise and to not bring heart into leadership has reached the end of its utility.

There's now incontrovertible proof that our common approach to leadership in America (the version that excludes the heart) has flamed out and is no longer sustainable. Never in the modern experience have our workers been so miserable, disengaged and under-performing against their full potential. This is killing business productivity. More than half of all workers in the U.S. *hate* their jobs. The major reason why: the needs of human beings (our employees) have evolved so profoundly that the leadership support they require in order to be fully engaged and productive is virtually unrecognizable compared to when our current leadership model was created.

Nearly 25 years ago, one of the country's most admired and enduring research firms began an ongoing study of worker satisfaction and engagement. They were first to discover that people have grown deeply unhappy in their work and, more importantly, the causes for the dissatisfaction. Their remarkable conclusion: people are crying out for heart. Workers cite the absence of concern, care and connection from their leaders as the primary reason for their discontent. They have the conviction that the people who lead them focus entirely on their own needs and goals all the while disrespecting what they need and are experiencing while on the job.

Additional research shows that workers want to feel valued and appreciated for the work they do. They want to be cared for individually and provided opportunities to develop and contribute at increasingly greater levels. Work has become exceedingly important to people and to their sense of meaning, significance and purpose in life. It's simply irrefutable that leadership in America is failing specifically because it lacks heart.

Separate from research on how our standard approach to leadership is affecting the performance of workers, I also wondered if science and even medicine could explain why feelings in the heart had so powerfully influenced my employees to excel. And what I learned very few people in business have ever heard.

For centuries, science believed the human heart played just one role in human life — as a blood pump. But new research has proved this understanding is entirely inaccurate. Instead, science now knows that the heart also is a source of extraordinary intelligence. Independent of the brain, it has its own logic that plays an enormous role in influencing human behavior. The heart also is where the human spirit resides and where people detect a sense of well being. *It's the heart, and not the mind, that drives human achievement; gestures that positively affect the heart naturally and reflexively inspire people to perform.*

We've been led to believe the mind is the highest form of intelligence possible and rarely think to consult the heart as we work to motivate people to perform. We've groomed our leaders to be intellectual, to subordinate feeling and to purposely marginalize their hearts. But this mind-driven belief system is flawed. It disconnects leaders from the people they lead and profoundly limits their effectiveness. This because emotions are an innate — and human — quality found in all people. Emotional energy is the true motivation of the human spirit; it's the force of life. Emotions create action and, with positive emotion, people are virtually limitless in what they can achieve.

What I've learned and concluded is that we need a new model of leadership for a new age — a paradigm that acknowledges the humanity — the hearts — in people. To be very clear and direct, this is by no means a feel good strategy. It's based on our collective understanding that it's rarely, if ever, an appeal to our *minds* that inspires any of us to do our greatest work. It's also based upon the understanding that when people flourish, organizations flourish. It can be condensed to these two sentences: "In every man there is a King. Speak to the King and the King will come forth".[1]

---

1   Scandinavian Proverb.

In Part I of this book, I will share all I learned from my research and will explain not only why we need an entirely new approach to leadership in America, but also why our leading more with our hearts has become so essential.

In Part II, I will introduce the four leadership practices which embody the idea of leading from the heart. These practices are easily adoptable and can be expected to inspire levels of achievement previously unimaginable.

CHAPTER 1

HOW WE LEAD IS FAILING:
THE NEED FOR HEART IN LEADERSHIP

To the business that we love, we eagerly arise, and go to with delight.
Shakespeare

Our Traditional Leadership Model is Archaic

Our common and traditional approach to leadership has not significantly evolved since the dawn of the industrial age. "When it comes to managing people in a work environment, we've always treated workers like any other input: squeeze as much out of them as possible and pay them as little as possible." According to Wharton Finance Professor, Alex Edmans, this idea was introduced nearly a century ago when the expansion of the U.S. economy largely was based on industrial machinery. Workers were required to perform relatively unchallenging tasks and were easily replaceable. Companies motivated workers primarily with money, paying by the piece to reward those who produced the most widgets. And so, if you think back a hundred years ago, the average worker went to work in order to meet their most basic human needs – to put food on the table and a roof over their heads. In exchange for their work, they received money, and money alone was entirely sufficient.

In a 1943 paper on human motivation, psychologist, Abraham Maslow, introduced the theory that people are motivated by a hierarchy of needs. "Maslow's Hierarchy" most often is depicted as a pyramid where the bottom level represents a person's most essential needs for food, water and shelter. His theory said that just as soon as these primary physical requirements are met, human needs progress to a second tier, the needs for safety and security[1]. And as people advance further up the pyramid, the needs become increasingly more social and psychological, and desire for connection, personal esteem and feelings of accomplishment take priority.

At the top of the pyramid, Maslow emphasized the importance of "self actualization," a process of growing and developing as a person to maximize one's full human potential. Maslow believed that people naturally and instinctively strive to fulfill all of the upper level needs – but only once their lower level needs have been met. So, once again, looking back a hundred years, the average worker wasn't thinking much if at all about the higher tiers of Maslow's pyramid. They weren't thinking about respect, the visibility of their efforts to the greater organization or, especially, any form of personal fulfillment.

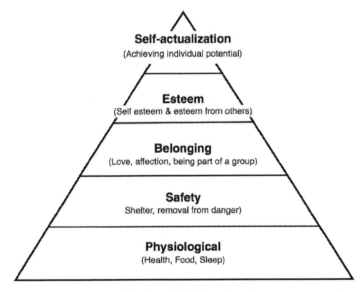

Self-actualization
(Achieving individual potential)

Esteem
(Self esteem & esteem from others)

Belonging
(Love, affection, being part of a group)

Safety
Shelter, removal from danger)

Physiological
(Health, Food, Sleep)

Maslow's Heirarchy

1   Interestingly, workers first formed labor unions to address the perceived lack of safety at their job sites.

The Business World – and Our Employees – Have Become Far More Complex

The overriding focus of leadership through the history of business has been to drive profit. And since workers historically had low expectations of what would be offered to them in exchange for their work (and more often were simply grateful to have an income), decisions on how to manage workers almost entirely were driven by the bottom line. Very little attention was placed on the welfare of workers – or to any of the higher level human needs Maslow identified. But as we fast forward to today's business world, shaped by rapidly changing technology and the far greater value of institutional knowledge, creative thinking, and sophisticated collaboration, the value of each employee has grown exponentially more important. These days, companies are producing more high quality products and services. They're focusing on innovation and unique differentiation and almost exclusively are looking at people, and not machines, to provide it.

Yet, in many significant ways, our approach to leadership has not adequately evolved to address and support the needs of the 21st Century worker. It ignores that workers no longer are as easily replaceable. It ignores how much businesses forfeit in terms of lost productivity and continuity when experienced employees leave. It ignores how greatly the needs of workers have changed and that people now seek – and "need" – much, much more from work than just a paycheck. Pay, as a motivator, in fact, no longer ranks number one for most people.

Being paid equitably will always be important as a driver of job satisfaction, engagement and productivity. But, over time, as people have become more affluent and their basic needs became satisfied, their higher level needs for things like respect, recognition and even fulfillment in the workplace have become much more important. And so now, people have progressed to the higher level needs – to the tip of Maslow's hierarchy – and far beyond pay (ironically, some people no longer even need to work but do so to fulfill higher needs). They now seek through their work the kind of actualization that Maslow outlined nearly seventy years ago.

Even More Complex Than We Might Ever Imagine
The Desire For Meaning, Purpose and Fulfillment From Work

A leadership axiom a century ago had it that people didn't want to work and would dodge it when not otherwise bossed around. The common belief at the time was that the only means of ensuring engagement was to reward people with pay tied directly to their level of productivity. Today, of course, most of us have the more enlightened view that people actually have an inclination to enjoy work and that performing one's work well can be intrinsically rewarding. Work, of course, has become far less tedious and monotonous for the most part, but what's really happened is that people have ascended in their needs and have landed on work as the place to fulfill them. People today have dreams and aspirations of work unimaginable a hundred years ago. While work will almost always be about a paycheck, the profound change of our times is that people have welded their sense of well being to their satisfaction with work. Research shows that the number of hours people work has increased over the past twenty years. With less down time for people, and with no change in the number of hours in a day, it's reasonable and even predictable that people would expect more from work in terms of personal fulfillment than ever before. But, even with so much of our lives invested in work, it still may be surprising that how happy we are at work now sets the stage for how happy we are in our *entire lives*.

According to a 2006 Europe-wide study conducted at the University of Aberdeen in Scotland, one of the world's oldest universities, job satisfaction has become the "most critical factor of life satisfaction and well being." The study concluded that one's career fulfillment doesn't merely influence happiness, it's actually become the top factor in a person's overall satisfaction with life. "This is over and above our satisfaction with family, leisure time, health, finance and social life," the report stated. The lead researcher, Professor Ioannis Theodossiou, explained it to me this way: *"I suppose that if one spends roughly two-thirds of his or her day at work, satisfaction with life will be heavily dependent upon job satisfaction."*

This is likely true, of course, but it's by no means the entire reason. What's also occurring is that people now are seeking more from work than perhaps ever before. In a direct response to how their lives were shaken and even unmoored by the "Great Recession," people across America are deep into the process of reassessing their values and re-ranking what's most important in life. Consequently, people now are looking at work very differently.

Time Magazine made this exact point in a March 2009 cover story titled, *"10 Ideas Changing the World Right Now."* Ranking number one on the list was the idea that our "jobs are the new assets." According to Time's writer, Barbara Kiviat, our society's collective consciousness is experiencing a dramatic shift to the extent that people – suddenly and seemingly all at once – have rediscovered their jobs as being the most valuable asset they can have. There's a massive change occurring in what people value most in their lives.

And Kiviat tells us why: the economic boom of the last decade distracted us from appreciating work. We allowed ourselves to get caught up with the ever rising values of our homes and stock investments; we directed our attention to all our perceived wealth. "People became mesmerized by how rich they were" is how Nobel Prize winning economist, Gary Becker, put it. It seemed to many people that every financial market would just keep going up and up. For a long time, they did. From 1999-2006, for example, housing prices more than doubled in the United States inspiring more people in our country's history to become a homeowner. And the Dow Jones industrial average, the bellwether index to the heart of our economy, nearly doubled in just five years – from October 2002 to October 2007. According to Kiviat, "the money the typical family had in the stock market soared from just 28% of financial assets in 1989 to a full 53% in 2007 as the percentage of families in the market jumped from 32% to 51%...Houses and stocks – those were the things we paid attention to...."

But, of course, now that we've seen how the story played out, we know it had a most unhappy ending. For many, much of their wealth proved illusory. Never since the Great Depression of the 1920's and 1930's has there been such a monumental reversal of fortunes:

- By mid-year 2011, home values across the country had fallen nearly 40% from peak levels.[2]
- In just two years, from 2009 to 2010, a record 2.2 million homeowners lost their homes to foreclosure.[3]
- Nearly 30% of all American homeowners now owe more on their mortgages than the current value of their homes.[4]
- Heading into 2011, retirement savings in the form of stock market values remained 20% less than when the market peaked in October 2007.[5]
- When the stock market bottomed out in March 2009, it had lost 13 years of gains.

According to the US News and World Report, after most recessions of the past 75 years, the economy quickly rebounded to pre-recession levels "erasing the memory of hard times." But this time has proved very different. The economic conditions the recession created are more fundamental and lasting – perhaps even permanent. For example, some analysts believe it could take a decade or more for home prices to reclaim their 2007 values, and even twice as long in the hardest hit "sand states" like Nevada, Arizona and Florida. And the economic setbacks have forced many Americans into a new austere reality where nearly two-thirds of us have reduced borrowing and spending. The reason, according to a 2010 Pew Research study, nearly half of Americans say they're in worse financial shape as a result of the downturn. More than

---

2   Source: Moodys.com
3   Source: RealtyTrac October, 2010
4   Zillow.com, February 2011
5   The stock market peaked in October, 2007 at 14,164. At year end, 2010, the Dow closed at 11,578. Even with the market's substantial rebound, most average investors missed out and didn't experience a significant recovery of retirement savings. After seeing so much of their net worth destroyed in the bear market, many stayed out of the market adopting a cash preservation strategy instead.

a third of workers aged 62 and older have had to postpone retirement because of financial setbacks. If anything, the economic meltdown has had the direct effect of ending the illusion of perceived security. For quite some time, people relied on structures of wealth (e.g. home values, investments and net worth) as points of stabilization of who they thought they were. With all of this breaking down, there's been a mass awakening. A lot of people all at once are saying "I've worked my ass off and this is all I have to show for it?"

But, if there is a silver lining, the whole ugly mess has forced people to ask themselves the bigger questions of life. As a result of this compulsory introspection, people are recalibrating what matters and what is of greatest value in life. Author, Judith Warner, calls it "*a resetting of all the clocks.*" People have changed what they value and now have the direct experience of knowing that dollars alone won't create abundance. All of a sudden, a huge part of society has had the same epiphany: there's nothing one can wear, drive, or own that can ever provide a sense of true and sustained fulfillment. People have come to face a huge void in their lives and are looking to fill it with something of far greater meaning. And this has led us all to look at work very, very differently.

Spotting the emerging trend, says Kiviat, is Dick Bolles, career expert and author of the world's best selling job hunting book, *What Color is Your Parachute:* "If as a society we turn back to work – if we dote on our jobs as much as we did our homes and our portfolios in an earlier era – then we'll have to start asking deeper questions about what we do." Written four decades ago, *What Color is Your Parachute* reappeared on the best seller list in 2009-2010. Bolles's book helps people figure out who they are as a person and what they most want out of life. Perhaps by seeing the number of books he's selling, Bolles is able to instinctively detect what's occurring in the American psyche and is stating what he already believes to be true. People are assessing whether the work they do – *and for whom*[6] – can provide them greater meaning and purpose. And Bolles is not alone is sensing where people are heading.

---

6   USA Today reported on March 28, 2011 that, a "morale meltdown," is causing more than one in three American workers to actively seek a new job.

In 1988, John Nesbitt and Patricia Aburdeen co-wrote *Megatrends: Ten New Directions Transforming Our Lives,* a New York Times best seller for over two years. In their book, the authors defined a "megatrend" as a large overarching direction that shapes our lives for a decade or more. Heading into the new millennium, the couple also wrote *Megatrends 2000.* Aburdeen now has gone solo to bring us current. In her book, *Megatrends 2010: Seven New Trends That Will Transform How You Work, Live and Invest,* she describes social, economic and even spiritual trends that are transforming people's expectations of work. In fact, Aburdeen is predicting that "The Power of Spirituality" will be the greatest megatrend of our current era.

Just like Kiviat, Aburdeen suggests that we've lost the sense of security we had in our lives and that the end of this illusion has led people to look back into themselves. The list of what ails us is long and pain provoking: the lingering threat of terrorism in the U.S. after 9/11, the prospect that upheaval in the Middle East will draw us into more wars, fears of Iran and North Korea's potential use of nuclear weapons, and the enduring effects of the economic meltdown all are weighing on us. People feel extremely vulnerable and insecure. This all comes at a time, Aburdeen suggests, when more and more people are seeking "wholeness and fulfillment" – greater meaning and a sense of well being in their life. People have been forced to reexamine their lives. And "when we find little security outside of ourselves, we are forced to search the heart and soul for new answers."[7]

Consequently, people are going through a process of deep introspection as they seek to identify what will give their life *authentic* meaning, and this is leading to a broad desire to connect with the universe, God, source – a quest for spirituality.

A 2007 poll conducted by AARP, one of the largest membership organizations in the United States (38 million people aged 50+), revealed that the number two New Year's resolution of its members was to become more spiritual. And a Gallup poll three years earlier

---

7   *Megatrends 2010,* p xxi

reported that 80% of all adults in the United States were feeling a need for spiritual growth compared to 40% just four years before.[8]

To be very clear, for most people, the need and desire for more spirituality has very little if anything to do with "religion" – the formal institution-based denominational worship of God – as it does with their heart. People may never use the word "heart" to describe their feelings, but it translates into decisions to seek out things that are meaningful in their lives – seeking to make their lives fulfilling and having a greater impact on the world around them. This difference is important as it affects people in their work lives. It's not at all about an open practice of formalized religion at work – most people neither want that nor believe it to be appropriate. Instead, a quest for spirituality at work means that people are seeking feelings of *personal significance*.

At its deepest level, this kind of fulfillment – contributing to one's greatest capacity and realizing one's purpose in life – is spiritual. To condense all this to a business bottom line: people (in all jobs and roles) want to feel that they matter and that the work they do matters. More than anything, they want to leave this planet fulfilled and not with a broken heart.

Aburdeen believes that people seeking a greater sense of purpose from work – a "quest for meaning" – already has reached critical mass. And she may have been the first to specify that our approach to leadership will require a significant overhaul in order to successfully match up with the new and profound needs in people. She's very clear in conveying that leaders whose intention is to respect, support, and develop people will become the new and productive model.

Let there be no doubt that this isn't just a phenomenon for the baby boom generation. Baby boomers, in fact, may just be late to the table given how overtly ambitious as a generation they have been. Workers just entering the workforce, the twenty to thirty-year-old children

8   Source: Institute of HeartMath.

of the boomers and so called "Millenial Generation," already have designed in a very different sense what they want their lifestyle to be. This generation needed no process or substantial life experience to bring them to this conclusion. Perhaps by observing the harried pace long maintained by their parents, they're instinctively seeking work that assures them of making satisfying contributions while having a life of greater balance. This generation already is upending the rigid and accepted norms of the workplace. From the get-go, they want flexible work schedules, more vacation days, and to be judged and rewarded based on the completion of their work – not on the number of hours spent on the job.

Traditional Leadership Has Not Evolved and Is Failing
Record Numbers of People Hate Their Jobs and Are Effectively Disengaged At Work

We know a century ago very little attention was given by leaders to the needs of workers. And if leadership succeeded in those days, it owes much to the fact that employees expected very little in return for work outside of pay. But now, of course, we know what people need and expect from work – the value exchange – has expanded significantly requiring leaders to suitably adapt.

But from the current perspective of the American worker, leaders in business and across all enterprises are nowhere near re-thinking, re-tooling or recreating a model of leadership which supports the new aspirations and spiritual needs in workers. Recent, comprehensive employee satisfaction and engagement studies performed by major universities and consulting firms provide unimpeachable proof that how we lead people today – how we seek to make people productive in the workplace – is so detached from the new reality that it's actually become a *destructive* influence, both to workers and to organizational effectiveness.

While it's clear from the data that record numbers of people now *hate* their jobs, this comes at a time when we've discovered most people are seeking to *thrive* at work. <u>The studies prove that our traditional leadership model has reached the end of its effectiveness. Workers across the country have grown widely disengaged and disheartened, and American productivity is being greatly undermined as a result.</u>

The Studies

The Conference Board of New York is a 95 year-old non-profit research and advisory firm well known for producing the country's "Consumer Price Index" and "Index of Leading Indicators." Since 1987, the organization also has been on the forefront in studying job satisfaction across America. Each year, researchers poll at least 5,000 US households ensuring study participation is consistently balanced tied to age, sex and geography. It's from the Conference Board that we learn empirically: people are really unhappy at work. In what is stunning news, employee satisfaction has been on a steep and steady decline every year since the study's inception. *Twenty-two consecutive years of declines in worker happiness.*

As a point of reference, when the Conference Board initiated the research, 61% of Americans expressed satisfaction with their current job. Now 61% isn't all that impressive, really, but it represents the glory days compared to how low that number subsequently has fallen. In 2009, at a time when many might have considered themselves fortunate just to have a job in a battered economy, the percentage of happy workers not only fell, it fell to an all-time low of just 45%. Thus, an astounding number of American workers, 55% – or more than one in every two – are discontented at work.

<u>US Job Satisfaction Hits a 22 Year Low:</u>

1987	61.1% of workers expressed satisfaction with their job.
1995	58.6%
1996	50.7%
2008	49.0%
2009	45.0%

When releasing the job satisfaction report in 2010, the Conference
Board put out the advance warning that the employee dissatisfaction
was in no meaningful way a result of a poor economy. Lynn Franco,
Research Director at the Conference Board, drove home the point
saying "through economic boom and bust during the past two
decades, our job satisfaction numbers have shown a consistent trend.
While one in ten Americans is now unemployed, their working
compatriots of all ages and incomes continue to grow increasingly
unhappy."

An ongoing Gallup poll concludes similarly. Over the past 25 years, a
period where there has been an enormous increase in prosperity, levels
of satisfaction with work nevertheless have declined in the U.S. In 1955,
44% of workers enjoyed their working hours more than anything else
they did. By 1999, only 16% did. It's unimaginable that this degree
of unhappiness isn't already having a severe impact on business and
organizational effectiveness, but if it has yet to occur, Franco added
her own warning: "the downward trend in job satisfaction could spell
trouble for the overall engagement of U.S. employees and ultimately
employee productivity."

In 2005, human resources consultants, Towers Perrin[9], began the
largest employee engagement study of its kind. They acquired feedback
from 85,000 people throughout the world-wide workforce including
workers at large and mid-sized companies in 16 countries. While the
Conference Board suggests the possibility that American business
productivity may be in jeopardy due to low employee job satisfaction,
Towers Perrin plainly believes the cancer already has spread to vital
organs.

The study found that just 21% of US workers are engaged in their jobs
and willing to go the extra mile for their organizations. Evidently
mindful of Maslow and the emerging higher needs in people, the
study authors offered this guidance: "there is a vast reserve of untapped
'employee performance potential' which can drive greater financial

---

9   Now named Towers Watson.

performance for any and all companies who make it their mission to actualize the other 79% of their workers."[10]

Donald Lowman, Managing Director of Towers Perrin's Human Resource Services at the time of the study, indicated that surveyed workers want very much to contribute more to the success of their organizations, but "they say their leaders and supervisors unintentionally put obstacles in their paths." The study found that highly engaged workers believe they can and do contribute more directly to business results than do less engaged workers. For example, 72% of the highly engaged workers believe they can positively affect customer service, versus only 27% of the disengaged. Highly engaged employees are also far less likely to leave for another job. According to Lowman, "the vast majority [of workers] are moderately engaged at best and a quarter of them are actively disengaged....This creates serious risks for companies since our research shows that companies with fewer engaged workers are far less likely to deliver on their growth agendas or achieve the kind of performance that shareholders demand."

Confirming again that money alone can't solve the problem (and what workers really are clamoring for is heart), the study states that employees remain frustrated and skeptical about senior management's ability to lead and inspire, but also in what they refer to as the "employment deal."[11] This "deal" goes well beyond pay raises, incentives and benefits. It includes emotional connections gained through things like fairness, career development and seeing how their work fits into the bigger picture of the organization. It's these kinds of thoughtful and personalized elements, the study cites, which often are more important than pay when people are making decisions to stay or leave a company. Towers Perrin reported that worker engagement scores have been low for quite a number of years noting employees are looking for guidance, direction, vision and clarity from both top management and their direct supervisors and "don't believe either is delivering to the extent they would like."

---

10   Towersperrin.com/hrservices
11   i.e. the value exchange.

While the Towers Perrin study maintains that "leaders and supervisors *unintentionally* put obstacles in the way of their employees," research conducted by the College of Business at Florida State University indicates that those obstructive efforts may very well be *intentional.*

The school surveyed over 700 men and women[12] working in a variety of jobs across the country and asked them how they were treated by their direct supervisor. The prime conclusion is that a remarkably high number of people believe they work for a bad boss.

At the root of the problem: too many leaders are entirely self-focused and lack any orientation for employee advocacy. And then there's a problem of trustworthiness. The 2007 study, published in Leadership Quarterly,[13] found that two in five bosses (39%) didn't keep their word (a mortal sin in leadership) and a nearly identical percentage failed to give credit to subordinates for work they had done. Making matters worse, many workers perceived their own manager as being a threat citing that bosses competed directly with them in order to make themselves look good. More than a quarter of workers said their supervisor bad-mouthed them in the presence of other workers or managers.

Consistent with the other studies, the research showed that the lack of healthy relationships (connection) between bosses and their subordinates had real consequences. Feeling undervalued and unappreciated, employees said they were less engaged, less productive and far less willing to show initiative by taking on additional tasks, working longer hours or weekends. And, once again, poor leadership was cited as a more important factor than pay in employee decisions to leave their organizations.

---

12   A statistically valid national sampling.
13   Fall 2007

CHAPTER 2

WHAT AMERICAN WORKERS SAY
LEADERS MUST DO TO RE-INSPIRE THEM

Hearts are not to be had as a gift. Hearts are to be earned.
William Butler Yeats

Not long ago, the Conference Board reported that a higher percentage of people enjoy their *commutes* to and from work more than the jobs that put them on the road. A lot of people, it seems, would just as well keep driving each morning than head into work. This grim revelation epitomizes what all three employee studies discovered: *people are undeniably unhappy at work* at a time when they're seeking much greater connection to it.

In representing the voice of workers across the country, the researchers were very effective in relating their distress. But they didn't go far enough. While the Florida State survey did pin down some very serious grievances, collectively, the studies missed the opportunity to identify the specific pain points driving worker dissatisfaction and, more importantly, to solicit guidance from workers on what leadership practices are required to re-inspire their full engagement.

Knowing that the Conference Board has been studying worker sentiment for over two decades, I wrote the organization to inquire if they had performed additional research beyond their own employee satisfaction study – something that might empirically identify solutions to all the discontent. In a matter of days, I had my response. Not only had they done the work, the study's author, John Gibbons, offered to present the findings to me.

As our meeting began, and I listened to Gibbons describe his professional background, I was impressed that his formative years were spent in business and that he had plenty of real world experience to influence his interpretation of research. Prior to joining the Conference Board and to becoming Director for Employee Engagement and Survey Services, he spent several years in an executive-level human resources role and had the experience of leading many people. With the mind-set of a senior business manager who is accountable for results, Gibbons sees it as his job to ensure the decline in job satisfaction in the U.S. is reversed. He's unquestionably dismayed by the trend, deeply believes the problem is fixable, and wants his research to be the catalyst for change.

With that goal in mind, and just minutes into our discussion, Gibbons wanted to make sure that I understood his firm's perspective on what's really causing all the unhappiness:

"What's disturbing is that we've seen a long and agonizing drop in job satisfaction since 1987 when the research started. In particular, we saw a steep drop in 2000, right before 9/11, and then just a gradual continuation of that trend through the last decade. **So, the decline is not associated to the current recession and is more endemic to how we manage people. Worker happiness scores only will improve when we make improvements to how we lead."**

Gibbons early assertion that we indeed have a leadership problem in our country made me eager to know how he had learned workers want the problem fixed. Displaying an impatient, bottom line orientation which misrepresented my enthusiastic interest, I blurted out this question:

"With happiness scores so low, what has the Conference Board determined leaders must do differently to re-inspire employees?"

To his credit, Gibbons wasn't inclined to provide a simple answer. He knew ahead of me that there was no silver bullet solution, but he also believed it was in my higher good to understand the *process* of how they arrived at their conclusions. In the deliberate, thorough, and thoughtful approach of a researcher, he explained his organization's methodology before presenting the key findings of his study.

Here's what I learned:

In addition to studying job satisfaction, the Conference Board performs separate research on employee *engagement* – a much more detailed and comprehensive study of how fully involved and enthusiastic people are with their work. "Engagement" is a force that drives human performance. When people are seen as "highly engaged," they're influenced to display initiative, approach work passionately and creatively and, essentially, to do all they can for their organization. When engagement is "low," of course, people feel less connected to their work and less compelled to put forth extra effort.

Gibbons explained that the process of assessing employee *engagement* is much more intricate compared to identifying job *satisfaction*. To determine if workers are happy, they're asked just one question. To identify someone's degree of engagement, researchers ask eight questions.

"We consider job satisfaction to be a cognitive[1] approach to looking at people's attachments to their work, or their organization or the people they work with. Engagement is more complex. It takes into consideration these same cognitive connections that people have with their jobs in addition to two other components:

    1. **Emotional** *attachments to work, and*

    2. **Behavioral** *responses to those attachments."*

---

1   i.e. based upon rational thought.

Gibbons provided examples to describe the kinds of questions they use in their study[2].

Emotional:
- Do you get a sense of pride out of associating with the organization where you work?
- Do you enjoy the relationships you have at work?
- Do you get a sense of fulfillment from your work?

Behavioral:
- Because of these cognitive and emotional attachments, do you intend to behave in a different way?
- Are you more inclined to apply discretionary effort at work?
- Are you inclined to stay working at your job even if you may have opportunities outside the organization as attractive as what you have today?

Engagement Is Significantly Influenced By Feelings

Evidenced by these questions, the Conference Board has discovered that a person's degree of engagement in the workplace is not just based on how they think about their job (cognitive), it's also significantly influenced by emotions and how they comprehensively *feel* about their job. One's emotional connection to work, that is, a person's *feelings* about their organization, boss and co-workers, and whether the work they do fulfills them, are seen as dominating determinants of engagement.

The word "emotional" is based upon the Latin word, "movere" meaning "to move." Thus, the word itself suggests a cause and effect. Emotions arouse feelings. Feelings influence movement – and behavior. Accordingly, how people are made to feel on their jobs, and whether they sense their own needs are being met, drives them to engaged or disengaged performance.

---

2   He was unable to provide all eight questions used.

The Top Conclusion From The Study: The Work We Assign People Is Uninspiring

As Gibbons transitioned our discussion to the results of his research, he told me there was one finding – the "headline" – that stood above all others as a key reason why engagement scores are falling: "There has been a dramatic drop in the interest employees have in the work they do every day." Separate and apart from how happy people were with their pay, benefits, commute to work, colleagues, bosses, etcetera, the one variable that dropped over the past 22 years was interest in the work itself."

In 1987, 70% of workers found their work interesting; in 2009 it had dropped to 51%.

After analyzing numerous variables in the feedback data, Gibbons and his team discovered that a number of them "collapsed" into a well defined category called *Job Design Issues.* "And job design issues," Gibbons noted, "are the most influential combination of drivers or catalysts for employee engagement – above everything else – for American respondents." The biggest reason why people are so unhappy and disengaged at work, the research shows, is "because we're designing their work very poorly."

What's Missing: Job Variety, Challenging Work Assignments And Visibility Of Employee Efforts To The Larger Enterprise

By "designing work poorly" Gibbons means that the work we ask people to do every day is lacking sufficient variety and challenge to make the job fulfilling. Consequently, worker's spirits have become dulled by routine and repetitive work assignments which afford little opportunity for growth, little if any chance for "self actualization." And Gibbons says another problem under the job design banner is that workers "lack visibility to the impact of the efforts they're applying on the job." Leaders aren't communicating how individual accomplishments impact the greater organization and, too often, fail to acknowledge the contributions their own people make. *Feeling* disconnected and disregarded, workers lose motivation and initiative. This all translates into low engagement.

Solving the job design issue is paramount to successfully re-engaging workers. "Obviously, no job is going to be perfect – and employees will never be great at everything," says Gibbons. "But when leaders assign work that inspires people, empathize with workers knowing some work will be boring or difficult, and dream up tough tasks as stretch assignments that will teach them and help them grow; I think you go a long way." The easiest and most thoughtful way to solve the job design issues problem is to do the untraditional and, per Gibbons, "build a personal relationship with each employee and purposely listen to what charges each of them up. Then, play up those aspects of the job that serves those passions."

Building employee engagement requires a degree of personal tailoring; leaders must identify what's important to each individual worker and put to use their unique and often hidden talents. Making time to honor and acknowledge people for their effort and contributions is the final requirement.

Big Rocks: Just Four Other Drivers, When Combined With Job Design Issues, Have The Greatest Impact On The Employee Experience

Addressing the job design issues will not entirely solve the engagement problem. But the Conference Board research has made the job for leaders easier by discovering that worker satisfaction in just four additional categories, or "drivers," explains 67% of the overall movement of employee engagement. This is a very powerful finding according to Gibbons. When workers have strong and positive feelings about these, their engagement will naturally and significantly improve.

The four are: "*Organizational Health*," "*Managerial Quality*," *Extrinsic Rewards*," and "*Workplace Readiness*." Sample questions asked of workers in each category include:

1. Organizational Health
   - Do the values expressed by my company resonate with my values?
   - Does the company have policies that apply to everyone equally?
   - Do I trust the senior management team to actually do what they say they're going to do and do they work with integrity?

2. Managerial Quality
   - How good of a manager do you have?
   - Does the manager care about you as a person?
   - Are they involved in your career development?
   - Do they give you clear direction on what you should be doing?
   - Do they give you recognition for a job well done?

3. Extrinsic Rewards
   - Are you satisfied with your pay and benefits?

4. Workplace Readiness
   - Do you have adequate equipment to do your job?
   - Do you have the necessary time to perform the task well or are you constantly up against a deadline you can't fulfill?
   - Do you have adequate work/life balance to set you up for success?

Because the Conference Board advises organizations around the world, they compared American employee engagement findings to those from other countries. What they found is that the exact combination of drivers — *the same 67%* — stays remarkably consistent across the world. The inference is what people need most to deeply connect to and fully engage at work is *universal*. The same five components of the work experience that are undermining worker engagement in America are essentially the same in every country. "The fluctuation is only two percentage points up or down when you go to China, Germany or Singapore," says Gibbons.

What *is* different is the order and weight that people from other cultures consider to be important. For example, in America, "job design" ranks highest in importance. But people in the UK place higher importance on organizational issues. "Do I work for an organization I believe in?" Do I work for a senior management team that expresses a strong degree of integrity?" In India, they found it is all about managerial relationships. "Are you immediately managed by someone who cares about you, who recognizes your contribution and who gives you clear direction?"

But regardless of which country they surveyed, the Conference Board made two extraordinary discoveries:

- **In every country, the job design component never dropped below number two in terms of importance. Job variety, challenge and visibility drive worker engagement world-wide. And,**

- **Across the world, pay and benefits never ranked higher than fifth.**

It was at this point in my conversation with Gibbons that I came to most appreciate his thoroughness. The insight that people in a work environment have essentially the same needs *across the planet* is amazing in itself. But so too is that fact that so much of what people everywhere need to thrive at work almost entirely boils down to emotions, feelings, and the heart.

> All over the world, people want to work for and contribute to the success of organizations whose values and practices they respect. They want to work for a trustworthy and empowering boss – someone who genuinely cares about them and ensures they're given opportunities to develop and stretch their capabilities. They want reasonable job variety – sufficient to utilize their unique talents – and to have their efforts recognized and sincerely appreciated. And all of these, across the world, take priority over pay.

In American business, so much investment and focus is given to motivating worker behavior tied to some form of pay and benefits. We've long believed that financial incentives and bonus plans were entirely sufficient to inspire human achievement in the workplace. Yet, the engagement study research shows why this is so misguided. People must be paid and they must be rewarded. But pay in the absence of a more caring form of leadership fails to inspire and, consequently, is ruinous to employee engagement.

Gibbons' Single Most Important Insight Into Leadership Effectiveness: "Love Your People"

At the onset of our meeting, Gibbons asked me to give him a quick synopsis of my ideas surrounding leadership and of the thesis of my book. I explained that I wanted to change the model of leadership in our country tied to what I learned from my own experience in successfully leading people. I had discovered certain leadership practices which affected people very deeply – at their core – and which influenced them to perform at extraordinary levels. The way we lead people is failing and, to restore its effectiveness, it is my thesis that we have to bring the heart back into leadership.

Hearing the word, "heart," Gibbons raised an immediate eyebrow and told me instinctively, and with unmistakable cynicism, that my idea may play well in California where I live, but not necessarily in the "rough and tumble," "sharp elbow" work environments like I'd find back east. We had just met, of course, and I didn't really give him much to go on in my answer. I believe he just wanted to caution me that some people will be more open to the idea of bringing heart into leadership than others and he assumed folks out west (Laid back? New agey?) would have greater tolerance for such ideas. Although I grew up in New York, managed people there for many years and didn't tend to agree with his remark at all, he graciously moved on.

The rest of our three-plus hours together, late on a Friday afternoon, were especially cordial. Heading into the meeting, I had no idea of how extremely generous with time and information he would be. We were at a natural conclusion point and as I started to thank him for all he had done for me, one additional question popped into my head, and I impulsively asked it:

"What is the single most important lesson or insight you have gleaned from all of the Conference Board's research that you most want American leaders to know?"

Given Gibbon's earlier bias and comments, not to mention his role as an objective researcher, his response simply astounded me – and he gave it to me without a moment's hesitation.

"The people who work for me all work fifty-plus hours a week. I believe when people make this kind of investment in the work, it's critical that they know they are part of something bigger than themselves. Make people believe that what they are doing is very important. Meaningful. But not only do I want them to believe this is the most important thing they can do right now, the other thing is that *"I just want to love them to pieces."*

Without a pause, he explained what he meant by the word "love."

"I think that when you have genuine appreciation for the people you lead, not only does this inspire you as a manager, but it also allows you to begin looking at them more than just the people who are performing the task you need fulfilled...We don't need to mother them, and we actually shouldn't, nor should we ever seek to become best friends. But it's a form of love I believe makes the difference between whether or not people feel the work they do matters and it is displayed in a variety of ways. It's work related."

CHAPTER 3

HAPPY WORKERS DRIVE *EXTRAORDINARILY* GREATER FINANCIAL PERFORMANCE

"...Management's job is to pay people....They have four categories: happy, satisfied, dissatisfied and disgusted. If they hit happy, they screwed up: They never want you happy. On the other hand, they don't want you disgusted so you quit. The sweet spot is somewhere between dissatisfied and disgusted."

Greg Lippmann
Head of Sub-prime Bond Sales at Deutsche Bank[1]

Is Business Really Better Off With Happy Workers?

One of the more cynical tenets of traditional leadership theory is that it's actually *desirable* to have some worker unhappiness. The assumption is that keeping people under a degree of constant tension is a more powerful driver of productivity and, ultimately, profitability. There's also the belief that when people are cared for to any extent they're likely to get soft in the middle – so sufficiently sated that motivation to work hard and produce is spoiled.

One thing we now know for certain is that people who feel "unhappy" at work have a proclivity to rebel. They've told researchers directly that they're purposely less productive, less engaged and far less willing to exert extra effort when they feel ineffectively or insincerely supported. If workers have a message for their leaders it's that they're far less dedicated when their hearts are not in their work.

---

1   Quoted in *The Big Short*, by Michael Lewis.

But what we've yet to resolve is whether people who say they *are* happy at work truly are any more productive than the discontented. Do engaged and happy workers really improve an organization's bottom line?

Where Employees Are Happiest: Fortune Magazine's *"100 Best Companies To Work For"*

In 1984, Fortune Magazine identified 100 companies which American workers ranked highest in areas such as job satisfaction, management effectiveness, and camaraderie. Fortune's now well known list of the *"100 Best Companies to Work For"* (i.e. where workers are happiest) was published for the first time that year – in book form – and then not again until 1993. In 1998, Fortune began updating its research every year and including it in special editions of its magazine.

Before I tell you which company ranked number one on Fortune's 2010 and 2011 list – the current best employer in America according to workers – let me say this: the 4,200 employees working at the company's North Carolina headquarters may very well be *the most indulged workers in our land.* Here's just a partial list of campus freebies and perks the company has chosen to give its employees:

- Free use of a 66,000 square feet gymnasium featuring tennis and basketball courts, weight room, billiards room, Pilates and yoga classes, sauna and heated pool.
- An onsite health-care clinic, staffed by physicians, nutritionists, physical therapists and psychologists – all entirely cost free.
- A hair salon and on-campus manicurist.
- On-site massage therapy.
- A subsidized cafeteria which prepares high quality take-home meals.
- Free snacks, Fresh Fruit Mondays and M&M Wednesdays.
- High quality child care provided at just $410 per month.
- *Unlimited* sick days.
- Flexible 35 hour work weeks.

Let's face it, most country clubs don't offer this many amenities. This is an extraordinary and unusual list of benefits. *What company would do this much for its workers, and why?*

The company is called Statistical Analysis Software, or SAS, the largest privately held software firm in the world. The legendary perks are the idea of Jim Goodnight, co-founder and CEO, who 33 years ago discovered that his acts of generosity toward SAS employees inspired them to work *harder* for him and to contribute *more* to the company. Sensing that "contented cows give more milk,"[2] Goodnight committed himself to doing more and more to create a highly supportive work environment.

If you take another look at the long, and presumably very costly, list of SAS employee perks, you might be inclined to judge the company's generosity as a good idea gone completely mad. That is, until you review its financial performance.

- SAS revenues have increased *every year* for 33 years running.
- Profit margins are in the double digits.
- (After the cost of all the perks) the company is very profitable earning $2.3 billion in 2009.
- Profits nearly doubled at the firm in just the last seven years.

Because the company is privately held and offers no stock options, SAS employees are not likely to get spectacularly rich through the appreciation of company stock.[3] Yet while people are paid fairly and are eligible for profit sharing (5-15% of base salary) and annual performance bonuses, it's really the company's work schedule flexibility and massive life-style accommodations which ensures SAS is able to attract and then retain the best workers. In fact, hardly anyone ever leaves SAS. Average employee tenure is 10 years and annual turnover of just 2% is by far the lowest in an industry which averages 22%. And every time the company does have an opening, they're able to strengthen

---

2   Fortune Magazine, February 8, 2010.
3   The company considered going public in 2000.

the organization; an estimated 40,000 people will apply for just 200 available positions this year.

Leadership Lessons From The Most Generous Perk Giver

There's no question that SAS is the paragon of employee perks and almost no other company in the country competes with their generosity.[4] And because how they treat workers is so unusual, and seemingly so over the top, we might be inclined to dismiss them as an incomparable outlier. But SAS's experience does indeed provide us with two exceptionally powerful insights:

1. *The experience SAS has with employee engagement contradicts the idea that cared for – even <u>extremely</u> well cared for – employees will lose their drive.*

SAS's experience proves it's just the opposite: "Some people may think that because SAS is family-friendly and has great benefits that we don't work hard," says SAS employee, Bev Brown. But, "people do work hard because they are motivated to take care of a company that takes care of them."[5] As evidence of that commitment, SAS workers take just an average of two sick days per year even though there's no policy or person keeping them from taking more. And all the campus conveniences make it easier for employees to work longer hours and to give their undivided attention to work.

When Goodnight began giving away M&M's every Wednesday, he had only seven employees to treat. But as the company expanded over the years and his perk programs became much more expensive, his inclination (as two-thirds owner and chief check writer) wasn't to cut back. Instead, he doubled down. He invested more and more – clearly with the understanding that doing so would be good for business. According to Goodnight, "the point of the benefits is to keep people. And if you keep people and make more people happy, they're going to

---

4   Google has purposely adopted SAS's model.

5   Fortune Magazine, February 8, 2010

make your customers happy. And if your customers are happy, they're going to make the company happy so it's sort of a triangle that you always have to keep in mind."[6]

2. *The second important lesson to be taken from SAS is a reiteration of what was inferred from the employee satisfaction and engagement studies:* **Money most often isn't the most powerful motivator of human achievement in the workplace. Feeling genuinely valued and cared for more often is.**

Consider, for example, one of SAS's on-site perks: on-site massages. It's really not clear why any employer would provide this. What the company could just as easily do is give their employees more salary instead of the cost of the massage. And offering massages isn't always seen as compelling because there are some people who just don't value them. So by giving people more pay, they can go use that money for whatever *they* would like to buy. SAS clearly has to realize that giving more pay is the more efficient and more traditional means of enriching employee lives yet it continues to provide massages. And the reason why, I believe, is because Goodnight long ago figured out that perks like massages are symbolic representations of how he and his company values its people. Because his perks affect how people feel, these perks are more powerful than extra cash as drivers of human performance. All of the trappings SAS provides, including massages, influence employees to sense they are cared for. The whole collection of perks exists as a constant reminder that SAS esteems them and that they matter. This care has the profound effect of getting people more deeply connected to SAS. These feelings tend to expand engagement and effort to levels well beyond what's normally expected leading to greater performance for the firm.

Culture And Leadership Practices: How Most *100 Best Companies To Work For* Win Over Employees.

SAS's munificence toward employees is quite atypical compared to most companies on Fortune's *"100 Best Companies To Work For"* list.

---

6   CBS Sunday Morning, February 28, 2010

Like SAS, the other 99 firms obviously regard employee satisfaction as a vital sign of organizational health, but rely more on organizational culture and leadership practices (vs. perks) to drive engagement. While most every company in America provides its workers some form of perks, some special and unique benefits, companies where employees are happiest have some obvious similarities with respect to how they treat people.

When announcing the 2010 best employers, Fortune included brief anecdotes about each company providing a small insight into what makes employees at these organizations so committed. What becomes clear from the reading of these is that the great places to work share five common traits:

1. They see employees as the heart of the company and place great focus on worker satisfaction and retention.[7]
2. They're committed to deep and ongoing development and mentoring.
3. Successes and people are routinely celebrated.
4. The firms reinforce the benefits of collaboration and team success.
5. They communicate effectively and frequently about individual and team achievements and how those impact their company.

Four Seasons Hotels: One of the *100 Best Companies To Work For* since 1998.

Undoubtedly, there are many companies on the Fortune best employer list which embody all five of these characteristics. Here's an example of how one company making the list puts them all together and inspires the highest worker devotion.

---

7   The stated company philosophy at Wegman's Food Markets (#3 on the 2010 and 2011 list) is: "We believe we can achieve our goals only if we *fulfill the needs* of our people."

Four Seasons Hotels is one of the priciest hotels in the world. People who check in to a Four Seasons property pay a lot of money to be treated like monarchs and, more often than not, it's the service provided by hotel employees which determines whether a guest experience is extraordinary. Over and above location and scenery, the Four Seasons differentiation is almost exclusively tied to how guests are treated.

When founding the company 40 years ago, CEO, Isadore Sharp, determined that the kind of service he wanted delivered had to be instinctive versus programmed. He wanted his employees to rely on their own wits rather than formula so that guest experiences could be more personalized and thus more exceptional. This business strategy inherently placed a lot of weight upon employee effectiveness and Sharp understood this. To ensure his employees were always the consistent embodiment of the Four Seasons standard, he decided he must treat his employees well: "Personal service is not something you can dictate as policy. It comes from the culture. How you treat your employees is how you expect them to treat your customers." Do unto others as you would have done unto you is the sincere company ethos.

Every new employee is intensively trained. They take part in a *three-month*-long regimen that teaches improvisational skills to prepare them for unique and unexpected guest interactions. Ensuring that skills are routinely developed and reinforced, the training never stops. With superior skills, employees are fully prepared to use their own individuality (empowerment) to independently solve guest problems or otherwise delight them.

The Four Seasons provides its share of perks. Employees build camaraderie by eating meals together, and are provided lockers and showers. But one benefit wows employees the most. After six months of employment, they are given a free three night stay at any Four Season's property. This is a wonderful gift, of course, but what's most impressive is the intentional thoughtfulness by which the Four Season's provides it. When employees use these rooms, they never are treated as workers but instead are considered genuine guests ("Welcome to the Four Seasons,

Mr. Jones"). It costs the company a few thousand dollars per employee but the investment inspires. Employees return from the experience feeling exceedingly rewarded and cared for. "You come back from those trips on fire," said one 17-year employee. "You want to do so much for the guest."[8] Average turnover at the Four Seasons is at least half the hotel industry norm. At some properties, it's in the single digits.

The Bottom Line: Workers Who Feel Cared For And Happy Generate Significantly And Consistently Greater Financial Performance

Alex Edmans is a thirty-one-year-old wunderkind who graduated at the top of his class at Oxford University's Merton College and was named a Fulbright Scholar while earning a PhD at the Sloan School of Management at MIT. He is now a professor of Finance at the Wharton Business School at the University of Pennsylvania. In a recently published research paper, *"Does the Stock Market Value Intangibles? Employee Satisfaction and Equity Prices,"* Edmans examined the stock market performance of companies with high employee satisfaction (Fortune's best employer list) and compared them with the broader market and peer firms within the same industry. I interviewed Professor Edmans and asked him what inspired him to do this research.

"Many companies say 'employees are our greatest assets' and people keep saying how the world is changing – 'the human asset is what matters, not the physical asset.' But this is something that companies can just be saying without actually meaning it. And there's a big debate as to whether employees actually add much to firm value because there was the old school philosophy which says the way to manage your workforce is to work them as hard as possible and to pay them as little as possible.

Because if you realize you are paying them less that will be better for shareholders. But even though if you stopped the average man on the street and told them that a company does better if the workers are happy, he'd say that is completely obvious. It's actually not an obvious relationship at all. It's something that

---

8   Fortune Magazine, February 1, 2008

has been hotly debated for many, many decades. The question which I think people have been unable to answer because something like employee satisfaction is intrinsically difficult to measure. So, as soon as I heard of the Fortune list, I thought this is way of testing this age old debate and to try to get some resolution to it."

And what did he prove? Happy and engaged workers generate far better market returns. His research shows that **the stock performance for "companies on Fortune Magazine's annual list of the "100 Best Companies to Work For" between 1984 and 2005 outperformed peer firms by 4% per year."** And Edmans emphasizes the significance of his own conclusion: "Four percent is a remarkably high advantage noting that hedge funds which beat the street by just 2% annually are consistently lauded as superstars."

To evaluate a long-term horizon for stock performance, Edmans went back to the earliest version of the Fortune list published as books in 1984 and 1993. Twenty-two years of a 4% greater stock performance is compelling validation for companies which long ago sought to engage and support their workforce. But as part of his research, Edmans analyzed the stock performance of all companies named to the list from 1998–2005[9] and found that the companies making the list had even greater performance above and beyond peers not named as a great place to work. **Over the eight year period, stock returns of the top 100 employers *annually* exceeded peers by a stunning 7-8% [10].**

"A more subtle implication of his study," Edmans told me, "goes to the nature of short-term thinking among corporate managers. Investing in employees often reduces earnings in the short term. And so leaders believing an investment in people (building human capital, building corporate culture) will pay off in the future often choose against making the investment. The concern is driven by managers who will argue it's not possible to credibly communicate to investors that profits might be

---

9   Fortune began updating the Top 100 list annually in 1998.
10   "Annualized alpha."

lower in one period in order to invest in employee satisfaction that may pay off in the future."

Edmans's research proves that by *not* making investments in people, companies under-perform against their true potential. Contrary to what many of us have always believed and acted upon, companies which find myriad ways to cultivate, honor and otherwise support the human needs of workers manage to consistently produce far greater returns for shareholders.

Authentic And Supportive Leadership – Not Perks – Is What Truly Inspires Worker Engagement

While writing this chapter, I had the concern that any discussion of Fortune Magazine's "*100 Best Companies To Work For*" list – especially all the lavish perks at SAS – could have the effect of misleading readers from what this book is really about. My decision to include this information deserves some final perspective.

In the first chapter, I showed how the traditional leadership model in America historically has been biased in the favor of the enterprise owner. Owners believed that improving the lives of workers represented a charge against their own earnings and, consequently, very infrequently made the investment. This narrow view, tied to fears of scarcity, is being invalidated by the practices of many companies, most notably those making Fortune's list. Contradicting longstanding beliefs, they're proving that there's a way to grow people *and* create greater affluence.

These organizations are advanced in their efforts at valuing and supporting employees and seem to know that their doing so has quite the enriching effect. What they're proving is that high employee engagement is the wonder drug. It helps companies retain and attract greater talent. When workers feel cared for they invest more of themselves into their jobs. They're inspired to serve customers better. Because their needs are being met, they instinctively put their heart into work. With so many people rowing at the same time, and in the same direction, companies are more profitable and return greater amounts to owners and shareholders. These companies are proving the effects of a much more sustainable and effective leadership model. A model which ensures all constituencies win and that creates prosperity, in the grandest sense, for all.

At the same time, I want to be very clear. I do not believe that adding some new perks to the company benefits plan will have any legitimate or sustained effect on worker satisfaction or engagement if that's the only change that is implemented. It's implausible that a company like SAS, for example, could give away massages in one moment and then treat their employees shabbily throughout the day. Perks like these, I believe, are gestures of care that reinforce numerous other leadership practices which support the well being of employees. While accessible cafeterias, hair salons and gyms all are wonderful in someone's work day, whether someone is truly happy and engaged at work, I believe, has little to do with access to a noon-time haircut and almost everything to do with how they're treated each day by their leader.

And that brings us back to what is the primary idea of this book: Leaders must individually change and adopt practices which honor and support the emerging needs in each person they supervise. More often than not, it's non-monetary, non-perk gestures that impact people most. Consistent and sincere efforts which make people feel safe, connected, understood, appreciated and significant affect people at their core and draw out greatness.

CHAPTER 4

ENGAGEMENT IS A DECISION OF THE HEART

The heart is seen as the seat of connection between the mind and the body forming a bridge between the two. The mind or spirit is housed in the heart, and the blood vessels are the communication channels that carry the heart's vital rhythmic messages throughout the body.

Chinese Medicine 2,500 A.D. [1]

Functioning as a pump – a truly remarkable one at that – the human heart moves blood around our bodies and beats an average of 70 times a minute, 4,200 times an hour and 100,000 times a day. That's an astonishing work load when you think about it, especially since it's accomplished with such consummate reliability and independence. In fact, all that pumping is regulated by the heart's own built-in pacemaker – a dedicated group of cells which generate the electrical impulses that makes the heart beat. Were the heart to have no other function than blood pump, it already would be the body's most important organ. The heart is the first to grow in an embryo – before the brain – and, while life can continue without a functioning brain, it ceases immediately once the heart has stopped. And so, a *lot* is riding on the heart.

For centuries, science and religion debated whether there was even more riding on the heart. Our ancient ancestors believed that the heart was imbued with a unique form of intelligence which profoundly influenced human behavior. They took this on faith and from their own direct experience, and argued that science is incapable of providing a complete view of reality. But science long ago won the debate. Science's

---

1   Institute of HeartMath

conclusion was that the heart's magnificence lies solely in its performance in circulating life sustaining oxygen and nutrients to every cell in the human body. And so science decreed that the heart neither influences nor has capacity for mental processes. Essentially, it asserted, the brain is where all the action is.

But in spite of science's conclusion, countless metaphors extolling expansive and even brain-like functionality of the heart have endured in our language – and in all of the world's languages. Owing to the Greeks, for example, "to learn it by heart" – to learn something well and lastingly – unquestionably ascribes brain-like memory to this blood pump. We must ask ourselves, if we truly believe the heart is only a pump, why have these myriad references endured? Have we not been entirely convinced?

History of How Ancient Civilizations Saw the Heart as the Seat of Wisdom

Dating back to ancient civilization, many cultures – Egyptians, Indians, and Chinese as examples – regarded the heart as being the seat of wisdom and where one's spirit resides. One of the oldest known references to this is found in the Bhagavad-Gita, Hindu scripture written between the 5th and 2nd centuries B.C., where Spirit is said to be "seated in the hearts of all beings." And there are innumerable examples through the ages of poets, philosophers and religious healers who also declared that the heart was the "seat of the soul."

In the 4th century B.C., when knowledge of anatomy and physiology was limited, Aristotle believed all human senses were sourced in the heart. He believed the heart was the primary seat of emotions and sensations because it housed the "central sense organ." In classical Greece and Rome, it was the heart rather than the brain that was seen as the source of mental processes including functions like thinking, memory and imagination. In the Book of Exodus, when God gave Moses the Ten Commandments, he told him his word of law was to be kept in the hearts (and not the brains) of men. The Bible also makes numerous references to the heart as being man's source of courage and wisdom – a belief shared by virtually all of the world's religions. Nevertheless, the broader view of the heart's functionality was largely based on speculation and without much scientific evidence. A more "scientific" view began emerging when Greek physicians first dissected the human body and discovered the nervous system.

Science Came to Refute the Ancients and Named the Brain as the Center of Intelligence

The second century Roman physician, Galen, was first to override the ancient's beliefs and concluded that the brain was the origin of speech, consciousness and intelligence. And in the 17th century, English doctor, William Harvey, offered proof that the heart was a pump providing continuous circulation of the blood. Western science went on to adopt such findings and has long validated that the brain is the true center of intelligence and home to all sensation and cognition. Science's bottom line: the brain is essentially in charge of everything; the heart is a pump, a hollow muscle that has no relationship to emotions, the soul or to intellect.

Yet considering how many words and expressions enter and exit our common vernacular year in and year out, innumerable references to powers of the heart have stood the test of time and remain very much alive in our language today. Despite science's firm and contradictory declarations, the ancient's view of the heart nevertheless remains deeply imbedded in our modern lives.

Indeed, our language suggests we believe the heart holds *extraordinary* power and influence in our lives. The heart is linked to:

Courage: lion-hearted, brave heart, Purple Heart, faint of heart
Enthusiasm and Passion: with all my heart, to lose heart
One's deepest feelings including joy and sadness: "You've touched my heart." "My heart is bursting with pride." "You have my most heartfelt thanks." "She's feeling tremendous heartache."

Kindness: open hearted, warm hearted. "She has our best interests at heart"

Compassion: coming from his heart, having your heart in the right place

What's Most Essential and Important: the heart of the matter, in your heart of hearts

Intellect: wise heart

Memory: to hold in our hearts, commit to heart

Imagination and Creativity: straight from your heart

Wisdom: "Follow your heart." "Let your heart be your guide." "My heart tells me this is the right thing to do."

Clearly, many terms and expressions that we relate to the heart convey a shared understanding and belief that the heart possesses some deep capability for thought, reasoning, perception, intuition and awareness. Despite all of science's protestations, we clearly seem to have the conviction that the heart *knows*.

Science Reverses Its Course: The Heart Isn't Just a Pump After All

Dr. Mimi Guarneri seems destined to have become a physician and, more specifically, a cardiologist. As a young girl, she watched her mother die from a sudden heart attack – an experience that led her to become "fascinated with hearts." She suffered another tragic loss when her brother drowned in a swimming accident and, yet another, when her own father succumbed to a heart attack at just 50 years old. Seemingly driven by a deep desire to minister to the hearts of others, very likely in order to heal her own, Mimi Guarneri graduated at the top of her class at SUNY Medical Center in New York and today is Founder/ Medical Director at the Scripps Center for Integrative Medicine in La Jolla, California.

Dr. Guarneri is also an author. In her recent book, *The Heart Speaks: A Cardiologist Reveals The Secret of Healing,* she describes groundbreaking research that, once and for all, confirms the heart is much more than a blood pump and is indeed a source of intelligence that often drives human decision making and behavior. The research effectively proves our ancient forbears had been right all along. But, more importantly, validates all that I learned through my direct experience in leading people: <u>what people feel in their hearts has tremendous influence over their motivation and performance in the workplace. The human heart is the driving force of human achievement.</u>

The Research

According to Guaneri, in the 1960's and 1970's researchers John and Beatrice Lacey were first to discover that the heart "was not just a pump but also an organ of great intelligence, with its own nervous system, decision making powers and connections to the brain. They found that the heart actually 'talks' with the brain, communicating with it in ways that affect how we perceive and react to the world. Over two decades of research, the Lacey's also found that the heart had its own logic, which often diverged from the command of the autonomic nervous system."[2]

In 1991, Dr. J. Andrew Armour introduced the concept of a functioning "heart brain," and showed that the heart has its own language and its own mind. In his book, *Neurocardiology,* co-edited with Dr. Jeffrey L. Nardell, Armour reveals that the heart, as a "little brain," has an elaborate circuitry that allows it to act independently of the cranial brain – to learn, remember, even sense and feel. Armour demonstrated that "with each beat the heart sends complex signals to our brain and other organs. These heart signals are capable of reaching higher brain centers, ultimately affecting our reasons and choices, our emotions and perceptions."

For the past two decades, the Institute of HeartMath has continued to research the intelligence of the heart adding to the work of the Laceys and Dr's. Armour and Nardell. According to Dr. Rollin McCraty, head

2   *The Heart Speaks,* p 156

researcher at HeartMath, "the heart has a mind that some might call the spirit, the higher self, intuition or the small voice within. How many times have you said to yourself, if only I had listened to my heart? By not listening, we often pay the price in time and energy in cleaning up the mess afterwards."[3]

All of the research confirms that the heart profoundly affects our judgments, awareness and intelligence, and that we very much make decisions with our heads *and* with our hearts.

Scientist, professor and author of 18 books, the late Dr. Paul Pearsall, conducted further research on the heart and on its relationship with the brain. On the very first page of his 1998 book, *The Heart's Code: Tapping the Wisdom of our Heart Energy,* Pearsall tells us that "as the human species developed its brain, it began to lose sight of its heart." He asserts that while science had long assumed the brain was in charge of everything and inherently made the heart beat, the heart actually has its own nervous system and has no need for the brain to direct it. But for many of us, he laments, the brain more often than not *does* tell us what to do. And consequently, we're so busy "doing, thinking and accomplishing" that we're seldom aware of the heart's intelligence.

Pearsall believed that the brain makes us individualistic – focused on our own achievements – while the heart needs interrelationship and connection. By being too brain driven, Pearsall makes clear, we ignore the fact that the heart provides its own insight and guidance that's "not ever in the brain's purview." In Pearsall's exceptionally brilliant book, he compares the intelligence and wisdom of the heart to the processing of the brain, and wants us to fully comprehend that the heart's way of thinking is "equally important to the brain's way of responding to the world." Some of his assertions:

- The brain thinks it's alone while the heart, with its humanness, knows it's not.

---

3   ibid, p 165

- The brain is always in a hurry seeking advancement, success and self survival; the heart wants bonds and connections that the brain won't slow down to establish.

- The heart knows that most achievements require intimate and mutually dependent connections with others.

- The brain is the source of intellectual intelligence (a brain that thinks) and the heart is the source of emotional intelligence (a brain that feels). Thus we must rely on head and heart as two sources of our intelligence.

Pearsall argues that we all too often ignore the heart's wisdom and thus forfeit ourselves in the process of deferring to the brain's incessant bidding for progress, movement and achievement. "If we allow our brain to think 'it is us' rather than a key part 'of us,' we cannot learn the true nature of what it means to be human. Survival of the fittest has come to mean survival of the smartest and most 'brainy'. As a result, the brain has been left free to 'do its Darwinian thing.' It has created an increasingly individualistic and separatist approach to living in which many of us end up feeling over-pressured and alone in our struggle for self-advancement and survival. In our striving to become more and more capable of controlling our world, we seem to have become much less connected within and with it."[4]

For many years, Pearsall experimented with his patients seeking to see where they instinctively perceived the physical location of their own human essence. I'll ask you to do what he asked of his patients: take one of your hands right now and use it to point to yourself. [5] If you are like most every patient Pearsall ever asked to do this, you pointed to the general area of your heart. And this clearly amused Pearsall who concluded "no matter how important it thinks it is, the brain that is coordinating the pointing movements seems to

---

4   *The Heart's Code*, p 16
5   Dr. Guarneri asks a similar question in her book: "Where do you feel love?"

know where a major component of the 'self' it shares with the body resides."[6]

In the *Heart's Code*, Dr. Pearsall presents the idea that the heart not only has the capacity to think and feel, but that heart cells even *remember*. As dramatic evidence that the heart is capable of storing memories, he provides several examples where heart-transplant recipients assumed personal characteristics – and even the knowledge – of their *donors*.

In one case, a young man who had been a vegetarian and extremely health conscious all his life, found himself suddenly desiring meat and fatty foods following the transplant. And the same patient, who always had loved heavy metal music, picked up his donor's passion for fifties rock and roll once he had the new heart.

But none of the stories is more fascinating than this one:

Dr. Pearsall was giving a speech to an international group of psychiatrists, psychologists and social workers where he shared his ideas about the heart's intelligence and profound influence in our lives. During the subsequent question and answer session, a psychiatrist came to the microphone and began sobbing as she tried to speak. When the words finally came out, she told him "I have a patient, an eight-year-old little girl who received the heart of a murdered ten-year-old-girl. Her mother brought her to me when she started screaming at night about her dreams of the man who had murdered her donor. She said her daughter knew who it was."[7]

Pearsall conducted several sessions of his own with the little girl discovering that he "could not deny the reality of what this child was telling me." Along with the girl's mother, Pearsall went to the police and, "using the descriptions from the little girl," they found the murderer. He later was convicted with the evidence the little girl

---

6   *The Heart's Code* p 23
7   ibid, p 7

provided. "Everything the little heart transplant recipient reported was completely accurate," said Pearsall.

Why This Research Is So Relevant To Leadership

We suspect that the best kept secret of successful leaders is love: Being in love with leading, with the people who do the work, with what the organizations produce and with those who honor the organization by using its work. Leadership is an affair of the heart, not the head. [8]

The Leadership Challenge
James Kouses and Barry Posner

As science has long overlooked the inherent intelligence of the human heart, the same can be said for leadership. With science historically conferring supreme stature to the brain, leadership long ago followed suit by over-esteeming the brain almost to the complete exclusion of the heart. Tied to the brain's urgings, leadership gives its unrelenting focus to activities, to the doing – to always wanting the ball moved down the field. The brain's way of leading, the old paradigm, takes things to excess. It's imbalanced.

Why? It ignores the hearts in people, the needs human beings have for meaningful connection and a sense of well being which, when absent, has the very real effect of dulling or even deadening motivation, engagement and passion for work.

When the brain gets down to business, it forgets that people doing all the work have hearts and inherently are beings with spirits which must be authentically tended to. We've long ignored how the heart can guide us personally as leaders but also how the hearts of those we lead need to be routinely engaged in the course of work. Dr. Pearsall believed that one's entire motivating life force comes from and is circulated by the heart. This being so, by our disregarding the hearts in others we're effectively precluded from connecting with people at their core.

To be fair, few of us ever were taught to appeal directly to an employee's heart. Most of us, in fact, were taught not to. And so, it seems, we made

---

8   *The Leadership Challenge*, p 305

a collective agreement to keep our relationships with subordinates "professional" and "business-like," code words for expressing our underlying belief that keeping heart out of the picture assures leaders of maintaining control and influence. Better yet, we believed we could make people more productive this way.

To correspond with these beliefs, few leadership-focused books I'm familiar with speak directly and deeply about the importance of tending to the hearts of subordinates. One book which does, however, is *The Leadership Challenge*, written by James Kouses and Barry Posner. Clearly on the vanguard when published 15 years ago, the now classic book introduces "Five Fundamental Practices of Exemplary Leadership." Named as one of the critical few: the practice of "Encouraging the Heart." To Kouses and Posner, the idea of encouraging the heart is limited to recognizing employee contributions and celebrating accomplishments. But through these practices alone, the authors believe, leaders will not only inspire phenomenal performance but will also, "elevate the human Spirit."[9]

The Leadership Challenge additionally expresses the enlightened view that the heart is a dimension of human nature that leadership cannot and must not ignore. The authors warn that "without employing people's hearts, organizations lose precious return on their investments in people."[10] And to make what's perhaps their most salient assertion on this same point, the authors quote Matthew Fox, author of *Reinvention of Work: A New Vision of Livelihood For Our Times,* who says "Work is an experience of the soul, our inner being....Work is an expression of the Spirit at work in the world through us."[11]

Noting how few leadership books ever mention the importance of the heart, I'm reminded of a conversation I had with Dr. Guaneri when she told me that what she was taught in medical school conflicted greatly with what she came to learn and understand through her own direct

9   ibid, p 132
10   ibid, p 41
11   ibid, p 41

experience treating heart patients. She explained that her medical school professors instructed her to perceive the human body not as a series of connected and interacting systems but instead as being comprised of distinct organs to be "owned" by a medical specialist. Science (along with the institutions which educated future doctors), in this "reductionist" point of view thus ignored all the metaphors that describe the heart and forgot that the human being is far more complex. "It also ignored what we appear to have always known, that we have feeling, we have intuition. The heart has intelligence that greatly influences human behavior".

After some experience as a cardiologist, Dr. Guaneri grew more inquisitive about the lives of her patients. "I started to look at my patients differently and asked the question, 'How can I help them deal with emotional issues, their responses to stressful situations that affect the heart'? How can I serve this person'?" And Dr. Guaneri believes modern medicine lost its way by focusing not on *health* care but instead on *disease* care. "We never talked about how does stress influence health? And even more, how does happiness and resiliency influence your health?"

The parallels to the way we lead people are striking: we cannot rely only on the brain to lead. Just as science forgot that the human being is far more complex than can be revealed in any medical metrics (blood pressure, cholesterol counts, etc.), as leaders, we've tended to ignore that the people who work for us are much more than their individual production measures and outputs.

If we believe that the best leaders elevate the spirit, we must acknowledge that the heart and spirit are one in the same. We must be willing to look at and really see the humanity – the human being – in every person who works for us. We must reject any lingering temptation to view employees simply as interchangeable parts – bodies without souls coming to work every day with a task to perform. Honoring, valuing, caring for and developing people individually, making people feel connected to work and its mission all create the sense of well being that people *need* to thrive. Essentially, we need to identify ways of improving the conditions of the hearts of those we lead as we now know with certainty that our doing so won't backfire on us or otherwise undermine our achievement. Our bringing the heart into balance with the brain in how we choose to treat people at work will lead us to having happier, much more engaged and productive employees.

A Healthier Way To Lead

If leading from the heart will make a leader more effective and his or her teams more productive, an added benefit is that leading this way also has been proved to be far healthier for the leader. Dr. Pearsall indicates that demonstrating care and concern for others, "giving love to others" has the not so ironic effect of leading to a healthier self. He calls the effect "healing the healer." Conversely, through the work of renowned researcher of human and organizational behavior, the late Dr. David McClelland, he shows that men who have a high need for control over people and events were two and one-half times more likely to develop heart disease by the time they were 50 years old. McClelland also discovered that the immune systems of "power seekers" were weaker than those who were more empowering.[12]

And Dr. Pearsall indicates that the heart in every human being is a sensing organ and has the amazing capability of accurately detecting the nature of energy coming from another's heart. This energy, he says, has an immediate, direct and profound effect (positively or negatively) on how people feel and react. Thus, people we lead cannot be fooled by false or unsupportive intentions. They can sense when a leader's concern is authentic. The good news is that care which is formed by genuine intention is felt by people to very positive effect.

According to Dr. Pearsall, we all can relate to the experience of meeting someone who gives off good or bad vibes. He describes a 92 year-old grandmother who, according to people around her, "brightens up a room as soon as she walks in." "Whenever I'm around her, I feel younger,

---

12　*The Heart's Code*, p 226-227

happier and more energetic," says her grandson. "She has such a good heart; you can feel it in your own heart." Now compare this energy to how a middle-aged accountant is perceived. "He's just a downer," people said. "He's always angry and tries to control everything, and when he can't, he just brings us all down. We know when he's down even before he walks in the door."[13]

Consequently, an important question for leaders is this: How do you make other people feel? How you make others *feel* is what people most remember about you – even if they form this memory unconsciously – and those feelings influence behavior long after the leader is in their presence. How you answer the question, according to Pearsall, describes how much of your own heart's energy you are giving to the people you lead. The more positive the heart energy, the healthier it is for not just for employees, but, importantly, for you.

Amor, Vincit Omnia. *(Love conquers all).*
Virgil (70 B.C. – 19 B.C.)

We now have scientific proof that the human heart has intelligence which profoundly influences human behavior. And this information is both game changing and paradigm breaking because it contradicts our long-standing opinion that leading more with and from the heart is inappropriate. Instead, it *confirms* that demonstrating care – giving heart to people in the broadest sense – is *essential* to maximizing human potential and achievement.

When I first began thinking about writing this book, I started coming across stories about unusual scientific experiments – all which showed that actions emanating from the heart (e.g. kindness, love and care) hold miraculous power throughout *all* living organisms. These illustrate the vital importance of connecting to the life force in human beings and, apparently, all things alive:

---

13   ibid, p 28

Using a high-powered microscope, Japanese researcher, Dr. Masaro Emoto, discovered that water when spoken to with kind and "loving" words shows brilliant, complex and even colorful snowflake patterns. Emoto, whose book, *The Message From Water*, has been translated into 45 languages, was first to photograph water crystals which formed after water was frozen. When the same water was exposed to what we would describe as being "negative" or unkind words, it formed incomplete, misshapen, uneven and asymmetrical patterns with dull color. Emoto's premise is that everything in nature has a vibration (energy) and words convert the vibration of nature into a sound. When asked what word would be most helpful to cleaning the world's natural bodies of water, Emoto said a combination of "thanks," "appreciation" and "gratitude"…creates the most powerful vibration of all".[14]

I tuned into CNN one night just as Dr. Deepak Chopra was describing an experiment involving hospital patients who just had returned home following extended treatment for a life-threatening condition. According to Dr. Chopra, nurses who had cared directly for these patients began calling them at home once a week. In each of these calls, the nurses told the patients that they had been thinking about them, missed seeing them, and wanted to hear how they were feeling and progressing. Noting this was an experiment, only half of the patients who left the hospital were called. However, the experiment was suspended soon after it started. The half of patients who never received calls from their former caretakers began dying in great disproportion to the patients who were called. The researchers quickly concluded it would be heartless and pointless to continue the experiment.

Finally, a study at Newcastle University in Great Britain recently discovered that the affectionate treatment of cattle – exhibited through the simple act of giving cows names like

Daisy, Rose and Buttercup – increased milk production by nearly six percent! According to Catherine Douglas who, with Peter Rowlinson, conducted the study, the "naming" is a reflection of the human's attitudes toward cows and how they behave around them. "Named cows," says Douglas, "are more often treated more nicely and well treated and happy cows make more milk." Ironically, the New York Times Magazine[15] spotted the idea that "cows when named make more milk" and, as an example of "ingenuity, invention and pioneering thinking," named it one of the world's best *new* ideas from 2009.

The conclusions from all of these studies are stunning, of course, but my guess is that you didn't find any of them all that surprising. It's really pretty clear that this and all the other recent research on the heart and its energy only confirms what we deep down have always believed. The wisdom of the ages – to include what always has been a fundamental teaching of all the world's religions and faiths – taught us that care, kindness and compassion, as forms of love, were essentially the most powerful and important things in our universe. Even if you never have milked a cow in your life, isn't there some form of wisdom inside of you that knew without the study that intentionally cared for cows naturally would have to be more productive? In the absence of any real "proof," this has been mostly philosophy even though those who put it into practice knew it to be true. But, as we know, we became a culture much more science based and more needing to prove things. So, over the past couple hundred of years especially, we grew to insist upon proving things and, more importantly, to discounting all that was un-proved. Keep in mind this is especially true in business. We became less trusting, cynical even, of these kinds of beliefs – ones tied to our own intuition, faith and even our own direct experience. But now, disagreements between science and religion are coming to an end. And in a superb irony, it is science that's now confirming there are two ways for us to know the world around us.

15   www.nytimes.com/projects/magazine/ideas/2009/#health

By definition, science focuses on experiment, measurement and *objective* evaluation to form its "reliable" conclusions. But another way of knowing the world is *subjective* or internal including gut feelings and intuition than cannot be easily explained but feel absolutely real nevertheless. It's this second form of understanding that many for so long (most especially in a business environment) have patently disregarded. Without any metrics or other reliable proof, scientists instinctively disavowed what people accepted on faith or by experience. And, we went right along relinquishing our authority to scientists.

The cow researchers provide a sad example of this. They studied 500 dairy farms across the United Kingdom and learned, not surprisingly, that farmers always had sensed that relating well with cows relaxed them and made them more milk. In the absence of conclusive proof, however, most farmers they studied chose to ignore their intuition and own experience. The researchers found that fewer than half of the cows ever had been named.

Can you imagine living on a small farm with animals to care for? You wouldn't think twice about naming *all* of them, most likely with thoughtfully chosen names to reflect their appearance or personality. Animals like these feel like extended members of the family. And, consequently, you'd be very much inclined to chat with them, pet them and otherwise make them feel special. Could you imagine having a bunch of nameless animals running around your farm, animals you depend on for milk, eggs – food you feed your family? But something unnatural occurs when we expand our farms and make them into a business enterprise. We ignore what we instinctively know and rationalize with ourselves that caring for our animals is no longer necessary or practical. The operation changes to a business driven by efficiency and we allow ourselves to lose complete sight of what's important and essential – and right. Our worst mistake is that we compromise our foundational and fundamental values (what we know in our hearts to be true) and delude ourselves into believing that efficiency alone will make our enterprises more productive and profitable. Making matters worse, our drive for efficiency inevitably leads us to conclude that taking time to name and relate well with cows is inherently *counter*productive. That spending brief moments in interaction can only lead to reduced revenue and profitability.

Skewed beliefs like these remain entrenched in business. As the cow researchers illustrated, it will be very challenging to convince some in business that bringing more heart into their operations won't just gum up the works. With a six percent jump in milk production – all derived from simple, un-costly gestures – it would seem very logical that *every* dairy farmer would get on board and name their cows. Not so, said the researchers. As an example, they cited a third generation dairy operator who says the research findings won't lead her to changing how she runs her business. "Everyone," she says, "has an ear tag and a number."

We've been operating for so long with these kinds of attitudes and convictions that it's realistic to expect certain continued skepticism, resistance and objection from some in business. And so to any remaining skeptics I offer more compelling evidence.

During the time I spent writing this book, I had the great fortune of being mentored by Bruce Creyer[16], co-founder of the Institute of HeartMath – a cutting-edge non-profit research organization founded 20 years ago to explore the then "budding concept that the human heart held a vast and previously unimagined intelligence."

In one of our conversations, I asked Bruce if there was any scientific reason why cows might respond so positively, so productively, to simply being named. I explained that the UK study demonstrated *that* it happened (i.e. cows produce more milk when named) but the researchers offered no scientific explanation for *why* it happened. What

16 Bruce today is President and CEO of HeartMath LLC, a for-profit arm of the Institute of HeartMath, which develops heart and stress related technology for the health care industry. Bruce and HeartMath co-founder, Doc Childre, co-authored "From Chaos to Coherence: The Power to Change Performance." Bruce also is adjunct professor at Stanford University's Graduate School of Business Executive Program.

I wondered was whether Bruce, through the work of his organization, knew the rest of the story. It turns out he did.

According to Bruce, here's why the simple gesture of naming a cow had the compelling affect of making the cow more productive.

"If you are calling that cow by a name, there's some kind of emotional connection that you have with that cow. Through HeartMath's research and the work of others we have learned that the heart is creating an energetic field. It's an electromagnetic field that extends outside the human body and is tangible. It's not an aura or something metaphysical. It's just like every electrical system [e.g. transformers] that creates fields. Well, that field changes depending upon our emotional state as evidenced by being physically close to somebody who's really upset and you can feel it. You take it on. Or, the opposite – being physically close to somebody who's in a very caring and appreciative state, and you feel that and take that on too. This confirms why you know when you are close to somebody who cares for you that it feels better being around someone who is frustrated, angry or impatient. Science is coming around to validate this. We've done a number of studies on animals [horses, dogs, etc.] and humans where the love of the human is translating to an actual physiological change in the animal."

"The heart of the dog and the boy or the trainer and the horse, for example, synchronize with the care from the human. So, the cow is feeling a connection when they hear you call their name. When you say 'Hey Bessie,' you're not saying this in thinking this is some lumbering animal; there's some kind of connection you have with this animal."

As we learned from Dr. Pearsall, Bruce also was clear in saying that no person is capable of faking that kind of connection, and that cows and other animals as much as humans very effectively sense (feel) any insincerity and lack of genuine intention: *"I'd also suspect that if you don't like Bessie, even if you use their name, there probably won't be a positive effect."*

The understanding that the human heart is much more than a pump and has profound influence over our lives has not yet reached the mainstream, particularly in business and in leadership. And yet, any leader who ever has experienced feelings of pride, joy or personal satisfaction in witnessing the catapulted progress and achievement of an employee they purposely helped and guided knows the power of it. Anyone who has built an empowered, actualized and productive team of people knows the power of it.

Business is unnecessarily frightened by the heart, but now the science and research make it clear that this kind of thinking is both misguided and misinformed. The debate is over and the final conclusion related to leadership is this: <u>To negate the heart is to negate what is essential in ourselves – and in all whom we lead.</u>

Gary Zukav, American Book Award winning author of "*The Dancing Wu Li Masters: An Overview of the New Physics,*" provides a concise understanding of why the heart has been for so long edged out and why we need to re-embrace it as a fundamental component to our humanity:

*Acceptance without proof is the fundamental characteristic of religion. Rejection without proof is the fundamental characteristic of science. In other words, religion has become a matter of the heart and science has become a matter of the mind. This regrettable state of affairs does not reflect the fact that physiologically, one cannot exist without the other. Mind and heart are only different aspects of **us**[17].*

---

17   *The Dancing Wu Li Masters*, p 97

PART II

THE FOUR PRACTICES OF
LEADING FROM THE HEART

Go to your bosom: knock there and ask your heart what it doth know.

Shakespeare

In Part I of this book, I've made the diagnosis that we have a serious leadership problem in America and that our traditional approach to motivating human behavior is entirely disconnected from what employees – *human beings* – actually need in order to perform to their greatest capacity.

In Part I, we've discovered that:

People Have Higher Needs That Leadership Is Ignoring

- There's a massive change occurring in society. The quest for individual meaning and purpose has hit critical mass. People are seeking personal fulfillment from their work and require a much greater sense of well being in order to thrive.

- Fewer than half of Americans are now happy at work. People feel undervalued, underappreciated and underdeveloped, and this has led to a significant reduction in engagement and worker productivity.

Engagement Is A Decision Of The Heart

- People work harder and contribute more to their organizations when their hearts are engaged. Leaders – and companies – which are succeeding in maximizing worker productivity today already have discovered that making employees feel valued and cared for is the most powerful way by far to motivate their achievement.

- Organizations which have the highest worker engagement share similar leadership attributes – an orientation which fuels the spirits in people:
  - They're highly selective in building cohesive teams.
  - They place great focus on employees and cultivate more personal relationships with them.
  - They develop and mentor everyone.
  - They acknowledge and celebrate all achievements.

Leading More From The Heart Is A More Effective And Sustainable Model

- It's been proved that companies where employees are more fully supported and thereby engaged enjoy phenomenal benefits. Employee turnover is consistently low, individual productivity is remarkably high, and financial returns make a quantum leap over those of less enlightened competitors.

- Leading with heart is not soft or sentimental – it's a necessary means of restoring worker commitment to the ambitions and goals of their organizations. Leadership of the heart is great for business and drives uncommon performance.

In Part II, I offer a prescription for restoring the effectiveness of American leadership – four practical leadership practices I have used and refined throughout my career to inspire incomparable employee achievement. What these practices have in common, of course, is that they, in some or many ways, help people to feel connected, understood, valued and significant – sensations which affect people in their core and ignite their spirits.

At first glance, these practices may appear basic or obvious. Please don't be misled. It's the consistent absence of these same four things that has led so many American workers to become so unhappy, disengaged and under-committed to their jobs. Adopting some or all of these potent practices may actually prove challenging. The idea of leading more with and from one's heart is by no means a technique. It requires great authenticity to be effective.

While I believe all leaders are capable of mastering all four practices, doing so for some will require a shift in perspective. I'll liken this to an American citizen who is moving permanently to Great Britain. They won't have to learn an entirely new language, but to succeed there they'll have to learn to drive on a different side of the street.

In the following chapters, I'll explain why each of the practices is so important, how they affect the hearts in people and why they drive such exceptional engagement. To share as much of my own insight into these practices as possible, I've made the chapters very personal. To illustrate how I've seen each practice successfully implemented, I share experiences from my life and career in addition to stories of famous and uncommonly successful leaders who seemed to instinctively lead from their hearts.

I spent the majority of my career in the financial services industry. Examples I use often include people in the role of teller, bank manager and investment consultant. Please realize I could only be intimate and effective by relating experiences with people I have actually led and worked with. Understand, however, that the effects of these four practices are *universal* and can be expected to be identical with all people you supervise regardless of job or industry.

These are the four practices of leading from the heart:

1. *Hire People With Heart*: **Build A Highly Engaged Team**

2. *Heart To Heart:* **Connect On A Personal Level**

3. *Empower The Heart:* **Maximize Employee Potential**

4. *Inspire The Heart:* **Value And Honor Achievements**

CHAPTER 5

HIRE PEOPLE WITH HEART:
BUILD A HIGHLY ENGAGED TEAM

Everyone has been made for some particular work and the desire for that work has been put in every heart.

Rumi, 13th Century

Sandlot Selection Process

There was a huge field across the street from my childhood home and boys from all over the neighborhood would meet there on summer evenings to play softball. These were pick-up games, not an organized league, and the first order of business was to choose-up sides. Typically, the two oldest boys appointed themselves captains before squaring off and selecting kids for their respective teams. The games we were about to play mattered none in any rankings – they just mattered in the moment.

Nevertheless, it was remarkable how thoughtful, disciplined and competitive these kids were in making their picks. These captains, men amongst boys at age thirteen and fourteen, displayed a determined ambition of building the stronger and better line up – even though their team would last for just one night. They fiercely wanted to win and saw that the choices they made before the game began would have lots to do with its outcome.

The selection process was simple enough. A quick game of rock, paper, scissors determined which captain picked first. Knowing you from the neighborhood, and having seen you play in past games, the captains looked you up and down and parlayed their knowledge of you into a hiring decision. Flashing rapidly through their minds: "Can he hit?" "Can he field?" "Is he fast?"

Everyone, of course, knew who the best players were and these kids got picked up first. And once chosen for a team, those boys had an immediate stake in who was picked next; they'd start yelling out names for their respective captains to consider: "Pick Gordon!" "Take Kevin!" Assembling these squads took just minutes, but there was a tremendous intensity and focus to it.

Once all the older and solid players had been taken, the captains changed their orientation in making all subsequent selections. With respect to younger and weaker boys, less focus was given to strengths and much more into determining which one was more likely to drop an important catch, strike out with players on base or otherwise blow it for the team. They were thinking about liabilities. Who would hurt their teams less?

If the captains had their way, none of the little kids like me would be chosen. The spirit of these games was that every boy there would make a team, but I remember, more than once, having a captain look me square in the eye and then purposely stall the process. In a moment of magical thinking, they would delay calling out my name all the while praying a bigger, stronger kid would miraculously appear so the other team would be forced to take me.

This ad-hoc selection process played out in my early youth many times and left a life-long impression that served me well in business. I learned from these older kids that building the best possible team begins with *intention*. Leaders must be conscious of the effect and impact every single hire will have on the performance of the team, on its momentum and on its future. Unlike what was forced upon them as children, these young captains taught me to choose people who could strengthen and contribute to the success of team, and to resist the temptation to *ever* make a hire just for the sake if getting an opening filled.

What's Obvious As A Kid Is Not So Obvious To Hiring Adults

My first job after college was as a management trainee for a large financial institution. My training was designed to last a full year and provided broad exposure to numerous aspects of banking. At the completion of the program, I was to be promoted into a leadership role – that's assuming I performed well all along the way.

My final assignment prior to being eligible for "placement" was to take on the role of manager at a large and busy bank branch. The "real" branch manager, Mike, was heading out on a three-week vacation and my challenge was to run the branch successfully in his absence.

Noting this was my final task as a trainee, I very much wanted to excel and to do my very best work. To that end, I drove out to the branch before Mike took off on his trip so we could review all of the responsibilities I'd be handling. The meeting went briskly. Mike answered all my questions, introduced me to the staff, and showed me performance reports that identified where I might give some special attention to help elevate the branch's achievement. I felt ready to take on my assignment.

Our meeting had ended and I was preparing to leave the branch when Mike called me back. He told me that he had forgotten an extra assignment that he hoped I'd have completed before he returned: he wanted me to hire three new employees – two tellers and a new accounts representative – to replace people who had just resigned.

In the moment, I was very excited to take on this added responsibility and to have the new workers on board upon Mike's return. Driving back to my office, however, it occurred to me how risky – even reckless – it was for Mike to have given me full responsibility for choosing people for *his* team. Coming to the branch for the very first time, I understood none of its challenges, had no knowledge of the people already on the staff, nor had any sense at all of the expertise and qualities that were most needed.

It was clear to me that Mike saw neither the risks associated with my making poor choices or even the value of taking time to provide his informed direction. In that moment, Mike had his mind on vacation – not on the long-term implications of the hiring decisions I was about to make.

Alternatively, I could have identified final candidates for Mike to meet, interview and select upon his return to work. Employees from other nearby branches could have been asked to fill in for a few weeks until this could occur. Instead, Mike insisted I rely on my own judgment – even though, after I was long gone, he would have to rely upon these same employees to help him achieve numerous and challenging sales targets and service goals. It was amazing to me that Mike failed to see the importance of having equity in every single hiring decision – the value of being able to convey to his employees that *he* picked them because *he* wanted them for his team and saw in them great talent. It occurred to me during this experience that young kids playing one game of softball took the hiring process much more seriously.

Find People Who Will Put Their Hearts Into Their Work

Drawing both from my childhood and professional experiences, by far the most important lesson I ever learned about building high performance teams is this: *Make it your intention that <u>every person</u> you select to your team will put their hearts into the work they're about to do.*

The more formative experiences of HeartMath co-founder, Doc Childre, underscore the importance of this practice. Inquisitive by nature, Childre spent much of his early adult years studying everything from vegetarianism to myriad spiritual practices. Including time he spent in the National Guard, and through other exploration and experimentation, he found a consistent theme: when it came to anything in his life that worked, it was because his heart was in it. His heart was connected to it. This was true of jobs, relationships, diets – when his heart was in it, it had a lot more staying power than when it wasn't.

Childre's insight provides exquisite guidance to anyone involved in hiring workers. Hire people with heart. Your objective is to find people who exhibit a clear passion for wanting to be part of what you do – people who display a genuine desire to perform a role and the talent or aptitude to succeed at it. You do this by being extremely thorough – *vigilant* – in the selection process knowing your goal each time out is to select people who will put the core of themselves into their work, not just a conceptual buy-in.

Everyone has some kind of work that they are good at – and that makes their heart sing. Too frequently, however, we put people into roles that don't match up to either those talents or passions. It's irrational to expect anything but half-hearted effort, commitment and effectiveness from someone who lacks genuine enthusiasm for the work they do all day. Never forget that there's a remarkable difference in the quality of one's craftsmanship when they love what they are doing.

And never doubt that there are people who are excited about and feel challenged by virtually every job there is to do in the world. When you realize there are people who passionately go about their day laying down asphalt, washing skyscraper windows, and nursing terminally ill patients, you realize that people are unique in what motivates them and in what roles represent the perfect fit. People are born with natural inclinations and it's the leader's job to match those to the appropriate role. Alain de Botton, Swiss author of *"The Pleasures and Sorrows of Work,"* suggests that way too many people ignore the seriousness of choosing one's work and, as a result, find themselves in positions that have little or no connection to their own aspirations and purpose. "I studied the world of career counseling and was amazed by just how casually people fall into jobs. Most of us are still in jobs chosen by our 22-year-old selves. We speak endlessly about waste: waste of energy, resources, of water. But the most shameful waste is of people's talents."[1] By leading from your heart, your objective is to help people grow, contribute and become maximized in their potential. Consequently, you must ensure no one on your watch ever "falls into" a position to which they are unnaturally suited.

It's been my professional experience that too many leaders greatly underestimate the downside – and upside – in making disciplined hiring decisions and, thus, fail to take the process seriously. Simply by hiring well – and by resisting the temptation to ever "settle" and put someone into a job where they didn't belong – I created a performance advantage for my teams that only became greater once people progressed into comfort and competency in their roles. Regardless of what position I needed to fill, my objective was to always find someone who would wholeheartedly commit to it and, thus, excel in it. Relying on a highly disciplined selection process, as the means to building an exceptional and highly engaged team, is the critically important first step toward achieving superior performance.

<u>Here Are Eight Steps To Follow When Making A Hiring Decision:</u>

1.   Define and Be Absolutely Clear On What Talent You Need

We've all heard the expression "opposites attract" and tend to believe there's a lot of truth to it. But consider your own personal relationships. Who are your friends? Who is your spouse or significant other? Are these people with whom you share little in common (opposites) or do you, in actuality, share many more similarities than differences? The truth is that we tend to surround ourselves with people who are like us. *People like people like themselves.*

The idea that people like people like themselves is something that you should circulate in your psyche every time you interview a candidate

---

1   Wall Street Journal, June 5, 2009

and find yourself really liking them. That's because we're also inclined to *hire* people like ourselves. And very often, hiring someone just like us – with the exact same talents, experience and personality – is entirely inappropriate for the role you are filling.

To avoid falling into this trap, you need to be very clear on what specific role for which you are hiring and, in advance of meeting with applicants, identify the skills it requires. One effective way of accomplishing this is to identify the top performers already in the job and determine what common traits lead them to excelling. Then, set your sights on finding people like *them.*

While you're at it, it's equally important to identify those people currently underperforming in the role, and define their limitations (e.g. skill-set, education, and demeanor). What common denominator deficiencies are restricting the success of your team's least effective members? Whatever you come up with become deal killers. In other words, avoid at all costs the temptation to hire anyone who doesn't have (or cannot quickly obtain) the skills and talents you need and want. Inevitably, there will be times when few immediate candidates have all you are looking for and you will be tempted to turn your head to the limitations. You must not bend or cave to this form of seduction! Whenever you settle for less, you move your team closer to mediocrity. Hold a position open longer, find temporary replacements – do everything you can to keep your standards high and to never ever compromise.

2. Always Seek To Improve the Strength and Talent on Your Team

When I was a regional manager overseeing a network of bank branches, one of my most talented and experienced branch managers, Lindy, called me and resigned. Our bank had just been acquired and Lindy learned that her above-average salary would suffer a massive cut under the new bank's compensation plan. Alarmed that she would be forfeiting something she worked nearly twenty-five years to earn, she joined a competitor which matched her salary.

The call was distressing to me. Lindy had been managing that same branch for two decades and was loved by all her customers. Because she brought great depth, maturity and competency to the job, it seemed a forgone conclusion that whoever replaced her could never match up to her. Ultimately, I decided to honor a top performing assistant manager on my team, Erin, and rewarded her with a promotion. Because she was much younger and far less seasoned than Lindy, I accepted that Erin logically would have a long learning curve before she would excel.

But this assumption was terribly misguided and taught me this invaluable lesson: *never limit in your mind what the possible outcomes can be*. Almost everything about Erin was different from Lindy. She was less outgoing, less sophisticated and less mature. But Erin had her own uniqueness and revealed during her interview that it had long been her aspiration to be the manager at this specific branch. Because of this unusual passion, she had given a tremendous amount of thought to what she would do with the branch were it ever to become hers to lead.

What I never really expected was how much this desire could translate into performance. Erin took the branch to higher levels of achievement in her first year as manager than had ever been accomplished. And she built her momentum almost immediately. This delighted me as much as it astonished me. Losing Lindy was tough for me and tough for our team – we loved and respected her. But Erin brought her own talents and personality to the role and excelled in ways I never imagined. We are inspired to strengthen our teams and organizations in every selection.

3. Look For Evidence of Ambition and Winning Ways

Educational Psychologist, Benjamin Bloom, examined the lives of some of America's most accomplished artists and scientists. In roles that we would assume intrinsically require natural ability, Bloom discovered it was personal drive and determination that led to their success. Certainly, these luminaries came to possess great "talent," but this developed over time – as a result of the love they had for what they were doing and a resolve for perfecting their craft.

A key objective in the interviewing process, then, is to identify people whose past achievements reveal these same special qualities. Other than when hiring for highly technical or senior positions, the qualities of ambition and persistence should rank above current skill level when building your teams.

To determine if a candidate has these qualities, you only need to look at their earlier work. Shakespeare said that "past is prologue." In other words, a candidate's achievements and successes (or lack thereof) in previous jobs is the best indicator of future performance. In the absence of a broad work history, a candidate's grade point average, athletic participation, involvement in organizations and employment while in school all provide indications of the motivations a candidate will bring to your team. Look for examples of unique achievements, examples of how they overcame challenges (drive and determination) to meet their goals.

When hiring, at every position, seek to identify winners – people who are passionate about what they do and find ways to excel. And there are plenty of winners out there. Winners take initiative. Winners get results. They want to grow, improve and to take on challenges. Winners want to contribute and winners strengthen others. Winners build and sustain momentum. Winners are fun to work with.

Because your objective as a leader will be to routinely develop the skills and talents of everyone on your team (including those you're about to hire), make it your goal to find people who have a clear history of putting their personal signatures on everything they do. Obviously, you need to hire people who have the fundamental and requisite skills for many positions you are filling. Yet, you should be very confident that you can teach people to do most jobs when they come to you with the spirit of desire and a track record of perseverance.

4. Interview With Purpose

Most companies provide managers with a recommended (or required) list of interview questions and the ones I have used at different organizations all were generally effective. At the same time, stock questions like these are never perfect and do not always elicit complete insight into the viability of candidates.

The following list of questions is provided as a supplement to whatever list you may be using and specifically will help you identify if your applicant has the high-priority qualities you require: **ambition, persistence and the heart to do the specific job for which you are hiring.**

To identify a candidate's ambition and desire to grow and achieve:
- Tell me about your greatest accomplishment this year.

- Do you set goals for yourself? If so, what are your immediate (short-term) goals? And, what would you like to accomplish in the next 2-3 years?

- How do you go about improving yourself?

To identify a candidate's persistence and ability to overcome obstacles:
- What happens when you don't achieve a goal you set for yourself?

- "Tell me about the most difficult challenge you have faced in your life. Describe how you handled it.

To identify job fit:
- What do you most enjoy about the work you are currently doing? What do you enjoy least?

- Tell me about a working experience when you were happiest.

5. Involve Your Team In The Selection Process

While we're all inclined to believe we are very skilled interviewers, I have learned to *never* trust my own opinion in making a job hire. I once had some small concerns about the experience of an investment consultant candidate, but otherwise thought she would be a really good fit in the role. To help me determine if the candidate's inexperience would prevent her from being successful, another consultant, Susie, offered to interview her. When the time came for us to debrief, I expected we would zero in on the experience question. Instead, Susie pointed out several attitudinal concerns that I had not picked up on in my meeting. I re-interviewed the candidate, immediately spotted the distasteful qualities and decided on the spot to never again go solo when adding someone to my team. A member of my team helped me avoid making a bad hire and showed me that more eyes and ears in the process produces more high quality selections.

This experience influenced me to begin involving some of my high-performing employees in all hiring decisions. After receiving thorough training in interviewing skills, these employees met as a small panel, interviewed finalist candidates and recommended which ones should be hired. And it wasn't long before I trusted their judgment. Candidates who succeeded through this gauntlet later proved to be consistently excellent in their jobs. My high-talent interviewers leveraged their own knowledge of what it takes to excel in the role and held their candidates to a very high standard. They also proved to be an excellent judge of whether the applicants would work well with other team members – a critical component of the process. The workers chosen for this special duty also saw the experience as a form of recognition. They felt respected by me, honored that I would trust them and, as a result, inspired to do their very best work. I also discovered that the panel employees would later go to the immediate aid of any struggling employee they helped bring on to the team.

Too often, leaders are anxious to get positions filled. My experience is that taking the time to be thorough, by including others from your team, and being patient in the process is greatly rewarded. Those you select can be expected to succeed for you today and well into the distant future.

6. Obtain Job Samples

According to Dan and Chip Heath, authors of *Made To Stick: Why Some Ideas Survive and Others Die,* our "official hiring process in America," the interview, is far less predictive of future job performance than a work sample. The Heath's believe we all know interviewing doesn't work that well but we continue to do it because we all think we're good at it. We see ourselves as Barbara Walters or Anderson Cooper – unfailingly uncovering the truth about our candidates. Psychologist Richard Nisbett calls this the "Interview Illusion." [2] Nisbett suggests it's illogical to think we can glean as much about a candidate in an hour long interview than we can by reviewing past accomplishments and statistics.

Imagine if a Major League baseball general manager selected players based only upon the result of a personal interview. It would be stupid to select a player based upon his interpersonal skills while ignoring all the previous work history that's readily available (e.g. life-time and current batting averages, fielding percentages, injury history et al). It's statistics like these, according to Nisbett, that are far better predictors of a player's ability and potential. Thus, acquiring job samples is far more effective than an interview.

"If you're hiring a sales person, have them sell you something." If you are hiring a graphic designer, have them show you samples of brochures and materials they previously designed – or have them design something new for you. Ask for sales reports, portfolio samples, performance reviews – anything that shows that they can do well the job for which you are hiring them.

If possible, the Heath's raise the bar even higher by suggesting candidates be tested on a skill most critical for success in the role. Example: one hiring manager gave a writing test to a Marketing Director candidate. The candidate had 20+ years of experience and interviewed beautifully in person. But, quite unexpectedly, she failed the writing test and wasn't offered the job.

---

2   Fast Company, June 2009

7. Before You Make an Offer, Give Finalists a Clear, Thorough and Honest Summary of Your Expectations and Job Duties

It might seem counterintuitive and risky, but I've always gone out of my way to disclose as much about the job – especially the down sides – before inviting someone to join my team. Early in my career, I hired some candidates whom *I* thought were an ideal fit only to see them leave a few months later. The reason they often gave me for their resignation was "the job turned out to be different than what I expected."

Because I am looking for people who want a long-term career with me and with my organization, experiencing this kind of turnover is extremely counter-productive. To solve it, I decided to lay everything on the line with candidates – before I ever made an offer. I decided to make certain that the person I wanted to hire understood all they were signing up for and, afterwards, could persuade me that they remained enthusiastic.

Go over the company's mission, its values, the key job duties and work hours. Show how they will be measured, evaluated and compensated. Explain your management style along with their opportunities for future career growth. Tell them how much travel is required; disclose expectations of weekend or evening hours, and any requirements to wear uniforms. Get it all out in the open. The tendency to avoid discussing these things up front almost always backfires. When new employees are on the job and come to learn what wasn't disclosed, trust in the leader is immediately and unnecessarily called in to question. We think we will risk losing a "great" candidate by revealing less attractive components of a job, but, in fact, we build tremendous trust by doing so. This behavior tells the employee that "we have no secrets" and that we believe the job with its pimples is still a great opportunity. Go so far as to let your final candidates spend some time (without you present) meeting with people on your team, especially those already in the same role the candidate will fill.

I have found it's really better to over-disclose then to under-disclose. If full disclosure leads to a candidate withdrawing, it's clearly better to lose them immediately instead of weeks or months after they join the team. Your goal is to ensure a new employee never has buyer's remorse and that they join you fully informed, and thus committed to the job and to the organization.

8. Listen To Your Heart When Making a Hiring Decision

When it comes to hiring, my advice is that your final step in the process is to consult your intuition – and to not only listen to it, but to trust it.

I once had an opportunity to hire a super-talented manager who had a reputation for producing extraordinary results. In fact, after she came on board, there were times when her branch not only ranked tops in my region, on a few occasions, it led the entire bank. But this manager also came with a reputation for being very selfish, bending rules and not getting along with peers. These tendencies didn't appear at first, but inevitably, word among her fellow managers was that she was unsupportive and often very uncooperative. And because collaboration was a core value of our team, the other managers on my team came to believe I was turning a blind eye to her insubordinate behavior. They accused me of holding her to a lower standard and of being seduced by her productivity. Making matters worse, the manager expressed to me that, because of all her unrivaled success, she was *entitled* to special treatment and wasn't required to conform to the team's ethos. It wasn't long thereafter that she became disruptive in meetings and began undermining the morale of an inordinately successful team.

I ended up having to terminate her employment but not without protracted discussions and involvement from Corporate Human Resources. The process took months (remembering her measurable performance was outstanding) and took a huge toll on my entire team. It also was embarrassing to me personally and the situation ultimately required the close attention of my boss. When I made the decision to hire her, a voice inside me told me that this manager had been a problem at her last bank and would very likely be one for me (past is prologue). But I turned down the volume of that voice and let my mind overrule my decision in the interest of having her superlative production. This was a horrible mistake. The experience was needlessly painful and was a great reminder for me to always trust my inner knowing. Your heart *knows*.

Final Thoughts

I once heard author, Brian Tracy, say that "the single greatest mistake a leader can make is a bad hire." His statement pierced me. Up until that time, I hadn't used much discipline in my hiring process and I could relate to the ugly, disruptive and often painful consequences of employee divorce. But Tracy's assertion also alerts us to the inverse: that this kind of pain and hardship is most often preventable and, there is tremendous upside when the leader makes a *good* hire. Consequently, I've learned that my employing a comprehensive interview methodology is the only means of consistently identifying true stars. Using a rigorous selection process makes even more sense when you consider the investment of time and energy you will be making in this new employee. Your commitment to building a personal relationship with them and to fostering their growth and development via mentoring and coaching is essentially wasted if your workers don't remain long enough for those efforts to pay dividends.

Studies show that personal interviews fail to provide the evidence that a work sample or skill test can provide. For that reason, hold candidates to the higher standard and request evidence of past performance and competency. But don't give up the interviews. Organizations still require them, of course, and striving to develop the interrogating skills of Columbo[3] remains a worthwhile ambition. In-person interviews also help you see if you connect with the person and that person with you. You get a sense after two or three meetings (some candidates won't get that far) whether there's a real match. Imagine yourself working with this person or the candidate interacting with co-workers and customers. Ask yourself: Do I feel good? Would I enjoy having this person on my team 5 or 10 years from now? Will they connect with the rest of my

---

3   Fictional television detective famous for his incessant questioning of suspects.

team? When making hiring decisions, leaders are smart to think long term – almost as if they were adding a member to their family.

It's also helpful to look at your disciplined interviewing process from the perspective of your applicant. Every step of the way, you are revealing a part of your personality, a glimpse into how you lead people. How you will lead *them*. While it's true today that jobs are more scarce, a healthy economy will inevitably return and people will again have greater choice where they work and for whom. You reveal much about your character by refusing to put someone into a role where it's clear there's no real fit. When you involve your team in the selection process, your applicant will see you as being secure in yourself, team oriented and empowering. By being truthful and complete in your explanation of job duties, you reveal yourself to be not just thorough, but unusually considerate, trustworthy and caring of others. The work you put into the selection process sets the example for what an employee can expect and sends the clear message that in working for you, they can anticipate not just succeeding – but thriving.

And once you do decide to make an offer and hire a candidate, you have a wonderful opportunity to honor your new employee by acknowledging them for how successful they were in the interview process. Commend their interpersonal skills and their work samples. By acknowledging all the hard work the candidate put into the entire process, you not only are expressing gratitude – grateful for having a highly qualified person join your team – but also are recognizing what really is their first real accomplishment: winning the job!

CHAPTER 6

HEART TO HEART:
CONNECT ON A PERSONAL LEVEL

If you want to know me, look inside your heart.
Lao Tsu 4th Century BC

To be effective today, the leader shoulders an almost sacred responsibility to create conditions that enable people to have happy and productive lives.
Peter Senge

From 2002 to 2010, San Diego State University raised its graduation rate from 44% to 61% – by far the highest improvement of any public University in the country. According to a study conducted by the Chronicle of Higher Education, SDSU's 17 point improvement came in a period when over a third of American Universities saw their graduation rates *decline*. The school's success was by no means an accident, and the process by which they so significantly improved student achievement has clear parallels to the practices of leading more from the heart.

As reported by the *San Diego Union-Tribune,*[1] the 114 year-old-school never paid much attention to its graduation rates. According to one University administrator, SDSU's faculty historically placed low expectations on its students and grew accustomed to the campus's enormous turnover. This finally changed when new University President, Stephen Weber, arrived on the scene; it was 1996 and the school was graduating just 38% of its student body.

---

1   December 26, 2010

Weber clearly saw SDSU's abysmal student success record as being a poor reflection of the school (not to mention a waste of human potential) and became personally determined to reverse the chronic trend. Understanding that the far majority of students enrolling at the University were not earning degrees, Weber was intentional in establishing a process which would support the achievement of *every* student on campus. Essentially, he went about raising graduation rates by doing two key things.

First, he raised the bar on student expectations by becoming far more disciplined and selective in the school's admissions. He sought to enroll students who were more committed to their education, better prepared for the rigors of the curriculum and thus more likely to succeed and even excel at SDSU.

Next, he purposefully set out to support these more qualified students by creating numerous "engagement and retention" efforts – a comprehensive approach to connecting with students individually and ensuring they knew the school cared about them and about their success as an SDSU student. This included the development of a mandatory summer orientation for all incoming freshmen and special support programs for at-risk students. And the University also created a "Compact Scholars Program," a once-a-week "class" for all first year students. In what effectively was regularly scheduled student outreach, the University saw to it that school counselors were able to routinely check in with students and see how they were managing all the demands of collegiate life. Counselors were able to provide guidance to students when they faced challenges and to help ensure these were managed before they severely impacted student performance. Even for kids sailing along and adapting well – the high achievers – the school made certain all of its students felt connected to the University and personally supported.

Weber's process for improving student achievement – as measured by graduation rates – is really quite enlightened. He effectively changed the paradigm of higher education which historically placed the burden of succeeding in college squarely on the backs of students. When I was in college 30 years ago, I rarely thought my university cared about me personally or was in any meaningful way concerned with whether or not I earned a degree. Whatever guidance I received, I almost always had to be the one to seek it. I most certainly had no one checking in with me to see how I was getting along in life.[2] But seeing how ineffective and indifferent San Diego State had been at getting its own students across the finish line, Weber decided an entirely new methodology was required. He concluded that once really qualified students came on campus, SDSU had a shared responsibility for ensuring they left with a degree.

Weber clearly understood that SDSU students would be reading all the books, writing all the papers and studying for all the exams. In other words, *as always*, students would be doing all of the work. But what he proved through his new system is that human achievement skyrockets when people are made to feel more supported and connected. He went out of his way to give students more individualized care and help to overcome obstacles standing in the way of their achievement. And by consistently demonstrating to students that they mattered and were valued, a far greater number of them graduated compared to any time in the school's history.

Breaking The Taboo: Leaders Who Make A Personal Connection With Employees Inspire Their Highest Achievement

Just as President Weber discovered that giving greater individual attention to college students dramatically improved their performance, I learned the same is true in business leadership. When I made time to more personally know the people who worked for me, it had the effect of significantly elevating their achievement. While it's long been engrained in us that *business* and *personal* require the same separation as church and state, here's the real truth:

---

2   My alma mater, University of California, San Diego, clearly does a better job today. Its 85% graduation rate now ranks seventh best of all U.S. public universities. They also gave me a superior education which more than makes up for their seeming indifference at the time.

If you want exceptional results from people who work for you, you need to make a personal connection with them.

One of the most enduring ideas to come from traditional leadership theory is that management must not be concerned with the personal issues affecting workers. The theory has us believing that connecting more personally with employees not only will complicate the leader-worker relationship, but it also will lead to our undoing. It's put us in irrational fear:

- We fear if we get personal with employees we will lose control.

- We believe our ability to implement change will be greatly compromised.

- We believe our devoting time to workers and their lives will hurt productivity and damage the bottom-line.

While there's no question that it's inappropriate for leaders to fraternize with subordinates and to otherwise become enmeshed in their private lives, out of fear, we have taken the idea to extreme. We fear our relating more personally to employees will undermine our effectiveness. In actuality, knowing your people more completely will make you a far more effective leader.

Much of this has to do with the fact that our employees *need* and want greater connection with their leader. That's not to suggest they want a deeply personal relationship. They don't at all. Our greatest impact with people is to gain insight into what motivates and inspires them in their lives. It also includes spending time with them for the purpose of discovering what may be limiting their highest effectiveness – even if that includes challenges in their own lives. On display is our desire to help every employee succeed and grow. People understand that we give time to things that are most important to us. And when people sense they matter and feel valued they instinctively become *more* engaged and *more* productive. It's a huge motivational force.

Studies have shown that people in positions of power are often focused on their own needs and goals while being unaware of what employees are feeling and experiencing. We need to change this orientation as we know impersonal leadership is failing workers. When I set out to meet with my employee individually, I had the following question running through my mind: *How much more effective and fulfilled can I make my employees by my gaining a greater understanding of the entire person – the human being?*

The Process Of Connecting On A Personal Level

For me, the process of connecting on a personal level meant spending uninterrupted time with every direct report on a consistent schedule where the meeting was exclusively focused on them. My objective in these heart-to-heart discussions was to discover anything that was challenging my employee's current performance (and to help resolve it if possible), to identify their short-term career ambitions, and to mutually create a development plan to help them achieve these ambitions. What follows is a detailed description of a six-step implementation process I used to make these discussions consistently productive and mutually worthwhile:

1. Clarify Your Motivations And Intentions For Holding One-On-One Meetings

Assuming you are not already holding one-one-one meetings with your employees – i.e. for the specific purpose of deepening your relationship and focusing on their professional growth – it's almost certain your team will have concerns about your motivations and intentions when you initiate them. Realize that feelings like these are very natural; it's human nature for people to fear what they don't yet fully understand. It is essential to the effectiveness of your initial meetings that you communicate well in advance all you seek to accomplish.

To introduce these meetings to my direct reports, I purposefully crafted an explanatory e-mail message and sent it out to all of them at the same time. This way, people could see that I was intending to meet with everyone and not just them.

In a brief but thorough note, I announced that I soon would be scheduling one hour one-on-one meetings and wanted to give them a preview of all we would be discussing. I expressed that the normal work day interactions too often failed to provide me adequate time to check in with each of them personally, or to focus on their career and personal development aspirations. I told them our having such discussions was very important to me and this, more than anything, was why I sought to fire-wall time for us to meet. I also explained that it was my intention to hold similar meetings every quarter[3] going forward to assure we would be able to more consistently connect with one another.

To make the very best of our time together, I asked them to spend some time thinking about how I could help them grow professionally (e.g. skill development, classes, special assignments) and to be prepared to discuss their career goals. I emphasized that the focus of our meeting would be upon them and not on current work targets. Nevertheless, I assured my team that we could still devote time to discussing any current concerns or questions they might have regarding the organization, their role, or on my direction and leadership. To conclude my communication, I expressed my excitement about being able to spend time with each of them like this.

The next time I had my team together in person, I reiterated my vision for these meetings, re-expressed my enthusiasm about spending this time with each of them, and solicited their questions and guidance on how we could make the meetings most worthwhile and effective. By giving them advance notice, discussing my objectives for the meetings in person (while everyone was together) and soliciting their ideas, my objective was, as much as possible, to eliminate ambiguity and to

---

3   I met every quarter with my direct reports and the next level down. Alternatively, these meetings can be held semi-annually or on a schedule you deem reasonable. Once you launch these discussions, your credibility as a leader goes on the line. You must be the one to ensure they are scheduled and held according to the promised schedule (i.e. every quarter) for trust to be maintained.

establish the necessary trust to ensure people weren't guarded or even closed off when the actual discussions began.

2. Launch The Discussion By Expressing Gratitude For Having Them On Your Team

Thinking I had done masterful work pre-communicating all we would discuss in these meetings,[4] I was completely caught off guard when my first scheduled employee seemed apprehensive as we sat down for our chat. Before I had a chance to say anything other than "hello," she very directly said to me: "So tell me again why you are having these meetings?"

Putting myself in her shoes in that moment, I quickly realized that I, too, would be feeling a bit anxious were I just about to have a conversation like this with *my* boss – especially if my boss had never reached out this way before. Understanding what I would be feeling in that moment – and needing to hear to become more trusting – I instinctively spoke from my heart. With complete sincerity, I told her that I felt tremendous gratitude for having her on my team and for all she did to support me and our organization. I told her that I valued her, cared about her personally, and wanted to do everything I could to help make her as effective as possible today all the while supporting her ambitions to grow in the short-term and long-term.

Immediately, as I said these things, I saw the effect it had on her. She visibly relaxed. She thanked me for saying this to her and told me how much she appreciated me wanting to help and support her like this. The remainder of our meeting was wonderful and extremely productive. My employee opened up, shared some personal issues and concerns, and then asked me to help grow her so she could assume greater responsibility in the firm. Based upon her aspirations and my belief in her ability to achieve them, we built a development plan for her to pursue and which I promised to support. I left the meeting feeling

---

4   The e-mail and team discussion remain necessary prerequisites to addressing most employee questions and concerns.

very optimistic about what I'd be able to achieve with all the others on my team whose meetings were to follow.

I did learn a few things in this first meeting that helped make all the others run more smoothly and effectively. First, I realized that the best way of initiating the discussion was to reiterate all that I had previously communicated about the purpose of the meeting and to establish a framework for what I hoped we would achieve in our time together. By providing this context, and then by seeking agreement, trust was established allowing the meetings to proceed as I had planned.

I also realized what a phenomenal opportunity it was for me to express to my employee directly the value I saw them adding to my team and organization. By providing that reassurance at the onset of an intimate discussion, I intentionally gave my employees authentic peace of mind about the pending discussion making a profound connection with them in the process. Obviously, what you say to each person will vary – and whatever you express must be fully merited – but telling someone who works for you that you appreciate them and want to help them grow is a powerful way to launch these conversations.

3.   Stick To The Agenda And Focus On Your Employee

These meetings have a specific purpose and easily can be derailed if you are undisciplined in managing the time and content. I think it's entirely appropriate that you tell each employee what you intend to discuss and the order in which you intend to follow.

Generally, your objective in these discussions is to accomplish the following, and in this sequence:

- To address any questions or concerns your employee brings to the meeting to discuss. (Be prepared to schedule more, and separate, time to address these if they're not quickly resolvable).

- To identify what's currently occurring in your employee's life that both supports and challenges them and their work performance. Seek also to identify the things in their lives that motivate them and are most important to them.

- To discover their short term and long term career aspirations and to direct them on a developmental plan.

- To use the final moments of the discussion to solicit suggestions on how you can improve as their leader.

There will be times during these discussions for you to do the speaking, but generally, your role is to get your employee talking while you listen intently. I found it best to begin the meeting by addressing the topics each employee deems important enough to bring to you before you transition to the intended focus of the meeting.

As you make this transition, I encourage you to inform your employee that you are doing so. In other words, let them know that you would like to now take the focus off current business issues and challenges and to place it upon them and on their personal development. By doing this, you create a natural segue – one that allows you to ask them two simple but important questions: "How are you doing?' and "How is your family?"

Way too often, we are so focused on the business at hand that we ignore asking these very basic questions. These *are* simple – but they are magical in their own right. By asking them, you are expressing your interest in your employee as a human being and in all that is occurring in their lives. And their answers will give you insight into how you might better personally support your employee to ensure their success on the job. There will be times when employees will reveal great joys in their lives (they're training for a marathon, buying a new home, getting married) or great challenges (their spouse lost their job, a parent has fallen ill). Your intention is to learn these things and to acknowledge their affects on your employee. This is not supposed to be an inquisition. Some employees will reveal more than others and you should never push, pry or otherwise insist they share greater detail. Just telling someone that you'd love to hear more about what's going on in their life opens the door for them to disclose what *they* think is appropriate. Trust me; you will learn plenty about each person just by displaying authentic interest.

Your role as leader is not to solve an employee's personal challenges (although there will be times when you can appropriately offer guidance). But expressing concern and empathy is another way of conveying to your employee that you care about their well being. Just saying that you care is extremely meaningful to people.

HeartMath recently reported that 75% of Americans describe their job as "stressful". They've also discovered that 60% of all workplace absenteeism is caused by stress. We've all been conditioned to believe that stress is intrinsic to work – a necessary evil – and so we invest little energy looking for its causes. According to Bruce Cryer, a lot of this stress is caused when people don't feel enough connection, appreciation and support from work. "People have a lot of stress going on in their lives – it could be caring for an aging parent, a chronically ill child, their own challenges. If the work environment is not supportive of their needs as a person and they have personal issues they are dealing with, you can't check those things at the door. Who can stop thinking about an ill child for eight hours? What human being would want that?" The lesson is that ignoring what is happening in people's lives is unnatural and is not only destructive to well being, it's destructive to productivity.

4. Discover Their Dreams And Aspirations

Few leaders I have worked for in my life ever took the time to tell me that they were looking out for my career growth and were routinely looking for ways to develop me. Much of this had to do with the fact that they weren't really concerned with these things and instead wanted me focused on accomplishing the business goals I had in front of me. It's been my experience that when you help people grow and fulfill their own dreams, the will perform for you in extraordinary ways.

Once again, simple, straightforward questions will elicit what you need to uncover:

- How do you feel about the progress you are making in your current role?

- What specific skills would you like to grow or develop?

- Have you given thought to what you might like to do next in your career and even further down the line?

- What are the things that I can do to help you achieve these dreams?

When I was a retail banking regional manager, I had a high performing branch manager tell me that she had aspirations of having a job like mine in the next year or two and wondered what I could do to prepare her. My immediate (and self-serving) reaction was that I didn't ever want her to leave my team. She was extraordinary and I didn't want to lose her. Reminding myself that people are only on loan to us as leaders and are never our personal property, my thoughts quickly went to how I could make her the best prepared candidate. Having been in the role for several years, I knew what skills were required and what experience she lacked. Rather than ask her for a plan, I built one for her. I had her shadow me and observe how I spent my days. I involved her in hiring new managers for my team and coached her on interviewing skills. I had her give presentations at our team meetings and build tactical sales plans for our region. While all these things prepared her to become a regional manager (she won the role and has excelled in it for nearly a decade), almost everything she did while developing herself supported the success of our region in some way. Better yet, the branch she led ranked among the top fifty out of over two thousand in the nationwide firm. While we're led to believe our helping people grow will be a distraction from the job at hand, never ever did she take her focus off the successful management of her branch.

In the context of this discussion, not everyone wants to grow beyond the role they have today. Not everyone wants to be a regional manager. But this doesn't mean that there are no growth opportunities. Everyone has areas where they struggle, skills that are weaker than others. Identifying ways of improving these will help your employee build greater self confidence and succeed at a higher level. Consider opportunities to design additional responsibilities (recall the importance of "job design") for your employees to deepen their enjoyment and routinely refresh their engagement in their role.

I once had a manager tell me that he had grown an interest in website design and asked if he could create a site for our region. My first reaction (human) was to fear that his doing so would over occupy his time. When he convinced me that he could do much of the work on his own time, and wanted to, I gave him permission. Soon, he had created a site which made available to his peers a lot of information and tools they needed and were unique to our region. His fellow managers loved what he produced and he grew deeper roots into his real job as a manager. Once again, his branch never ever suffered – it actually hit its highest levels of achievement in the months he spent putting the site together.

It's entirely appropriate that you give your employees direct and honest feedback on where they can grow and improve. I have found that these meetings invite greater honesty since people really want to know how they can perform better. Noting this meeting is *not* a performance review, you can help your employee by identifying specific weakness areas that you have observed. While doing so, however, remember the words of author, Anne Lamott: "You don't always have to chop with the sword of truth. You can point with it." Pick one or two skills to work on and make sure you have your employee's agreement. Your process should be to identify areas of weakness, target them, and keep the focus alive until they're improved.

5. Demonstrate Your Intent To Grow Them And Develop A Plan

After I had conducted these meetings with my direct reports for a few consecutive quarters, it dawned on me that my holding similar meetings with the assistant managers (the next level down) could help me to strengthen my bench all the while helping me to develop tighter relationships with important members of my team. Using all the same steps as before, I informed my assistant managers of my intention to come out to meet with them and sent out a calendar.

In one of these discussions, I met with Maureen. Prior to my working with her, Maureen already had been an assistant manager for several years. When we discussed her aspirations, she told me that she not only hoped to be promoted, but specifically wanted to become the manager at the branch where she currently was working – it was located in her home town. Understanding that managers often stayed years in one branch, Maureen told me she was willing to wait until the current manager transferred or left the organization.

What Maureen had no way of knowing at the time was that I was about to terminate the employment of her manager[5] creating the very opening she dreamed of. I could have been a hero a few days later by promoting Maureen, but I felt she was unprepared and insufficiently developed to take on greater responsibility.

I can't remember in my entire career seeing anyone as disappointed and upset as Maureen was when I informed her that I was assigning someone else to manage the branch. I understood in the moment that there probably was no one on the planet who wanted to lead this branch as much as she did. Maureen was consistently professional but managed to convey her perspective that it was hypocritical of me to come out and meet with her, get to know her dreams and aspirations, and then quickly betray all that by selecting someone else for the role. Ouch!

---

5   Due to serious bank policy violations.

A few days later, I went back out and met with Maureen for the purpose of doing two things. First, I told her that her previous – and now terminated – manager had insufficiently trained her and that I wanted her fully competent before taking on a branch manager assignment. Second, I identified the skills she lacked and worked with her on developing a plan for her to follow to acquire them. I brought the new manager into the meeting and directed her to support and coach Maureen's growth so that, should she ever leave, Maureen would be ready.

The plot thickened less than a year later when Maureen's new manager suddenly was called back east to tend to an ill parent. The dream job was once again available. And I still didn't think Maureen was ready.

When I met with Maureen, I pulled out the development plan we had created a year earlier. I pointed out which skills she had newly mastered but also the ones she had left to tackle. Acknowledging she still had work to do, Maureen understood, with obvious grief, that she wasn't yet ready for the promotion. As I had done before, I committed to continue helping her develop and encouraged her to never give up on her dream. My doing this had the effect of keeping her very much engaged rather than focused on her disappointments. Another year later, the manager who I had assigned to the branch in place of Maureen asked to take on a larger, more challenging branch. I willingly obliged – she not only deserved it, but she also had fully trained Maureen to assume the manager role. It was an emotional moment for both of us when I finally promoted Maureen. Nine years later, she's still the leader (and thriving) at her home town bank branch.

6. Use The Discussions To Grow Your Own Leadership Effectiveness

Before your meeting concludes, you have a wonderful opportunity to learn from your employee how they think you can be a more effective leader. You have to develop the stomach for accepting some direct feedback, but taking this final step in the meeting not only will greatly strengthen the relationship you have with your employees (they'll be impressed by your courage), you'll also identify what leadership shortfalls most require addressing. I grew more as a leader by acting on subordinate guidance than from almost any other source.

Just as you're winding things down, inform your employee that you have one more thing that you would like to accomplish. You would like to get their feedback on how you are doing as their boss. Transition quickly to asking this question: "Please tell me one thing that you think I am doing *well* as a leader."

Be prepared to hear that you should be America's next President. Wanting to please you, but also to reward you for taking valuable time to help them grow, they will shower you with praise. But while hearing all the good is indeed valuable and reinforcing, you are asking this question in order to get on to the next one. After your employee has ended their extolling you for all your leadership expertise, tell them you have one more thing to ask: "Please now tell me one thing I can do *better.*"

Your employees will almost always be reluctant to give you any bad news, but you must persist to learn their insights. You may have to remind them that they already have praised you and so their providing one current weakness should necessarily follow. Make sure you are taking notes – and get ready.

You may be surprised, but your employees will have given this question a lot of thought long before you ask it. Their answers might make you wince and they might even hurt. But it will make you so much more effective as a leader if you take the feedback and act upon it in a way that shows your employee and team that you took it all seriously and worked to improve. It will also inspire enormous loyalty and support. Acknowledging your own humanity and shortfalls also builds enormous trust for the next time you ask your employees to open up to you.

CHAPTER 7

EMPOWER THE HEART:
MAXIMIZE EMPLOYEE POTENTIAL

If we did all the things we are capable of, we would literally astound ourselves.

Thomas Edison

A leader takes people where they want to go. A great leader takes people where they don't necessarily want to go but ought to be.

Rosalynn Carter

The Windsor Knot – Part I

When I was a ten-year-old Cub Scout, I had to learn to tie a Windsor knot. The challenge in front of me was to follow the instructions in my scouting handbook and self-teach my way into a merit badge. My big problem was that the assignment played to none of my strengths. At that young age, I already knew I was seriously challenged to comprehend dotted-lined, three dimensional "how to" illustrations of any kind. Once I opened my handbook and saw the convoluted diagram of how one supposedly makes a Windsor knot, the idea of my ever learning it seemed entirely hopeless.

But that's not to say I had given up on getting the badge. No, I still wanted that – but mostly because I didn't want to be the only kid not to get one. All the boys in my scouting den had super-involved parents (the kind who wore adult-sized Cub Scout attire to our meetings) and there was no question in my mind that every kid would be sufficiently tutored to master the complexities of the large-knotted tie were they to need the help.

But at my house things were different. Because my father was so characteristically unsupportive, impatient and confrontational, I was terrified to ask him to teach me. This presented another problem. According to the Cub Scouting organization, before I could earn my merit badge, I needed a parent to sign my handbook and attest that I had indeed learned the skill. With my mother now deceased, this requirement was *forcing* me to go to my dad. Deciding I'd be smarter to maneuver around my father's usual volatility and to not ask for the help I really needed, I concluded my only legitimate course of action was to devise a way to just get his signature.

On the night before our den's next meeting – when badges would be presented – I hatched a plan to wait until it was way past my bedtime and to then ask my father for a quick signature. The premise for my scheme was that it would be very late and that he'd be instinctively inclined to scribble his name in my book in order to get me back into bed. That was my hope. At the appointed hour, I came downstairs in my pajamas and found my father sitting in the living room. Believing speed was my friend, I had the handbook opened and pen in hand. As I gave both of these to him, I hurriedly explained that I was getting a new badge at the next evening's meeting and needed his signature to make it official. In the moment, I expected him to say something to me but he didn't utter a word. Instead, as if he were a train conductor routinely punching a passenger's ticket, he took the book from my hands, looked at the page briefly and signed away. He then closed the book, handed it back to me and told me to get up to bed.

Holy cow – I had planned this out perfectly! At that very second, I had tremendous feelings of relief, but also feelings of fear that things could go south for as long as I remained with my father. So, I high-tailed it out of the room.

For the next fifteen or so seconds, I was under the illusion that everything had worked out wonderfully. But my perspective changed the moment my father called me back into the room. I hadn't even made it up the stairs. Just as soon as I heard my name, I had an instinctively sick feeling which recalled the collective times when his anger was on overload and he mercilessly attacked. As I turned around and headed back, I expected he would scream at me for my attempted deception. Accordingly, I braced for his worst. But he had a very different and unpredictable response that night. In the few moments I was gone, he had removed the dress tie from his own neck. Once I was in the room, he displayed none of the expected rage. Instead, he handed me the tie and simply said "How 'bout you show me how to tie a Windsor knot."

I immediately came clean. I told him I didn't have a clue as to how to tie that knot and blabbered something about needing a degree in mechanical engineering to interpret the directions in my handbook. (Probably now in tears), I told him I didn't want to be the only one of my friends to not get their badge.

On this one occasion, he was the ideal father who responded with care, patience and palpable kindness. Relying on his own knowledge and expertise, he proceeded to teach me how to tie the knot. Standing behind me, he placed the silk around my neck and methodically proceeded through the steps; I watched as his process resulted in my wearing the first Windsor knot I'd ever seen. He then untied it and painstakingly walked me through the sequence over and over until I was fully proficient in tying the tie on my own. To prove to me that I had mastered the knot – and had overcome my fears and doubts – he had me tie it with my eyes closed. Already well practiced, I had no problem doing it. The knot I made while effectively blindfolded was a thing of beauty.

It was, of course, hugely satisfying to me that I had acquired this new skill – and even more that I had learned it from my father. Now very happy and believing my lesson was over, I handed my father his tie. To my amazement, however, he remained engaged and told me that he had something else to show me. My father explained that few people in business wore the bulky "Full Windsor" anymore and that it had become more stylish to wear a smaller-knotted tie, the "Half Windsor." Ignoring that it was already extremely late – and a school night – he explained that I should also know how to tie a Half-Windsor and proceeded to show me.

Having been made to feel very confident in tying the Full Windsor, I learned to tie the new knot with ease. On my first solo trip, I nailed the Half Windsor and took myself to the mirror to admire my handiwork. While I was there, my father told me to stay put; he had one little trick he wanted to show me. Standing behind me again, with the tie still around my neck, he pinched the knot from the inside while then also pulling the knot tight. He called the resulting detail a "dimple" and explained that, as a finishing touch, it not only made the tie look magnificent but it also was the "mark if a very professional and conscientious man."

On the next night's scout meeting, all the boys lined up and, one-by-one, had their handbooks inspected by our den father. Just as I predicted, every kid earned their badge. When our little award ceremony was over and we had recited the Pledge of Allegiance, we were scheduled to paint bird houses we all had made at the prior meeting. Taking the direction of one of the parents, we went down into the basement, found our project and then sat down against the wall to await further instruction.

The paint brushes were all set out for us and it seemed as if we were about to be reminded to be careful – and to not spill – before being set loose to put the first coat on our crafts. Instead, our den father, standing up in front of us and searching our faces, surprised us by asking "Who would like to show us how to tie a Windsor knot?" Supercharged (and extremely heartened) from the night before, I raised my hand and ran up before most kids had even heard the question. Feeling enormously self-assured after being so meticulously taught, I flaunted my new skills: Full Windsor. Half Windsor. Dimple. It was an incredibly gratifying moment – mostly because, for the first time in my life, I knew I was more effectively prepared to perform a task than any other person in the room.

I remember this experience in such vivid detail because it was the *only* time in my entire life when my father took an interest in teaching me a skill he already had mastered. This is not at all an exaggeration. I honestly cannot recall a single other time when he saddled up to me to review my homework, discuss my classes or advise me on the myriad topics where he already was an expert. Not once again. While he had exceedingly high expectations of me and demanded that I earn high grades, excel in sports and distinguish myself amongst my peers, he did almost nothing during my entire eighteen-year childhood to strengthen my ability or confidence to perform. And so, in the absence of his guidance and direction, I was consistently left to build my abilities through trial and error – by far the slowest, most frustrating and inefficient road to effectiveness or mastery of any skill. Not surprisingly, in the absence of any kind of assistance and support to solidify my competencies, I very often failed to meet his lofty expectations. Ironically, my mediocre achievements led him to being disappointed and frustrated in *me*.

It always struck me as a colossal waste of my own human potential that I learned almost nothing substantial from all his rich experience and hard-earned knowledge. A long-lingering question I have asked myself is "How much more effective and successful could I have been made to be – in all aspects of my life – had my father purposely and generously shared the insight, information and wherewithal he had already mastered? I've given a lot of thought to how powerfully he could have influenced my growth, confidence and success had he just shared what he already knew – his skills, wisdom and tricks of the trade.

Consider this man's biography. As a child, he lived through World War I. He endured the Great Depression. He was a Commander in the Navy during World War II. By the time I was born, he had become one of the highest ranking executives at General Electric. What did he electively teach me from all of this compelling life experience? Full Windsor. Half Windsor. Dimple. This one lesson was all he ever really chose to contribute to help accelerate my life's learning curve.

By now, I'm hoping you are wondering why he didn't share – why he hoarded all his useful and exquisite knowledge instead of seeking to build me up? When my father was a young boy, his parents divorced and he subsequently had very infrequent contact with his own dad over all the years to come. The experience forced my father to grow up quickly. Throughout his childhood, he worked to support his mother and sister and missed out on a lot of normal and enjoyable childhood experiences. Having to work so hard to get ahead in life led my father to becoming deeply resentful of others. Rather than be proud of all he accomplished and overcame, he begrudged people whom he perceived had succeeded simply because they hadn't faced similar challenges. More than anything, my father's early experiences influenced him to compete directly with everyone else in the universe tied to deep-seated feelings of *lack* – a warped belief that someone else's success and achievements inherently took something away from his own. Consequently, my father saw everyone as an adversary, a competitor and a threat. This included me.

When I was a high school freshman and sophomore, I pole-vaulted. None of our coaches knew much about the sport and so I experimented, and through trial and error, I learned on my own the skills to effectively compete. My father also had been a pole-vaulter – a great one. While at the University of Minnesota, he set the school and state record and only missed out on the Olympics due to injury. Despite having this unusual experience and talent in the sport, never once did he offer me his tutelage as a means to helping me succeed.

Scarcity and Abundance

> *The sage does not hoard and thereby bestows. The more one lives for others, the greater his life. The more one gives to others, the greater his abundance.*
>
> *Lao-Tzu*
> *Tao Te Ching, 6th Century B.C.*

While you might be inclined to perceive my father as an outlier, I believe he's really an archetype – a quite common example – of leaders in our society who go to work every day fearing for their jobs and influenced to neglect or even disregard the needs of others. It's an old underlying type of energy and rhetoric that pervades a lot of companies and influences leaders to compete – and to not support the success of the very people they lead. In its worst manifestation, these leaders become cut-throat and entirely self-serving because they have a feeling of lack that says "I have to be this way in order to survive." At the root of this fear is a pervasive belief that we live in a world where *everything* is limited – a world where if another person's light grows brighter, theirs must naturally and equivalently grow dimmer. It's a feeling of scarcity – an entrenched conviction that there is never enough to go around – and it leads people into concluding "Every man for himself."

In his book, *The 7 Habits of Highly Effective People,* Stephen Covey called this belief system a "scarcity mentality." Others refer to it as a "poverty consciousness." Call it what you will, both terms define a state of mind that yields a very destructive form of leadership. Very often, leaders who believe in scarcity aren't even consciously aware. But the fear-based beliefs which circulate in their psyches include:

- Since opportunity is limited, I need to compete with others. I have to get mine because there won't be enough for everyone.

- By teaching others, by sharing my knowledge and expertise, I will inherently diminish myself and become less powerful.

- My helping others to grow, develop and progress will lead to them catapulting over me in some way – recognition, compensation, title and career opportunities.

Consequently, whenever a leader suffers from a poverty consciousness, it leads them (again, often unconsciously) to thwart the growth of people – to hold back information and expertise for themselves.

The far more healthier – and accurate – belief system is what Covey called an "abundance mentality," a confidence that there is truly enough of everything. When leaders bring an abundance mentality to their roles, they believe:

- The universe has no limits on the number of people who can be successful.

- Everyone, not just a few, can achieve, grow and thrive. I can enjoy the success of others with equanimity.

- When you give of yourself – of your time, your knowledge, your help – others inevitably give more.

According to Covey, to possess an abundance mentality, leaders inherently must have a deep inner sense of personal worth, self confidence and security. In fact, it's often the lack of self belief that influences leaders into the baseless fears of scarcity and loss – and to not fully develop the capacity of others.

Here's what I know to be true: *when leaders value themselves while also valuing others, they're able to create extraordinary results.* Leaders with an abundance mentality fully understand that they're expanded – that their own lights glow brighter and brighter – when they help others to grow and achieve. Leading from the heart is about proactively strengthening others, teaching others and building people into their full human potential and highest levels of achievement. In order for leaders to support their employees in this way, they must be willing to forego fear – and to give up some of their power – with the understanding that their doing so will produce the incomparable. Helping to develop people who work for you subtracts nothing from you and, through universal laws of nature, is instead rewarded by phenomenal achievement. In the words of St. Mark, *"The measure you give will be the measure you get, and still more will be given to you."*[1]

---

1   Mark 4:24

The Added Benefits of Developing People

We know that traditional leadership theory was entirely unconcerned with maximizing human potential. A hundred years ago, people were taught to perform a specific task and little more. What's endured from this model is a hyper-focus on execution and the concern that time spent developing people – especially in ways that aren't current job related – will compromise productivity. Even when we know better, when we believe taking time to further enhance the effectiveness of our employees will serve us and our organizations well, we cave in the face of a busy day or an immediate goal to meet. In the moment, we overlook that every day is hectic and that new goals and challenges will await us as soon as we conquer the ones in front of us. And so, we build and reinforce the habit of putting aside plans we had to coach and teach our employees under the delusion that we'll try again soon – we'll get to it next month. As leaders, we need much greater discipline and must also shed aside any remaining vestiges of traditional management theory once and for all.

We know from the Conference Board and other research organizations that we can no longer neglect the higher needs in people – for professional growth and talent building – if we are to expect comprehensive engagement and productivity. While we all have the lingering anxiety that spending time investing in the development of people will *halt* the production line, employee output only accelerates when people feel supported in their expansion and career progression.

The bottom line: *Leaders will excel when everyone is in an ongoing process of broadening and deepening their capabilities.*

Here are just a few other reasons why purposely growing employees is so important:

People Have Enormous Potential To Do And Achieve More

One of the most satisfying discoveries I made as a leader is that people have far greater potential to contribute than we allow ourselves to imagine. We pigeon-hole people, judge them too quickly and overlook the greater capacity that lies inside them. People are almost never fully maximized in their potential; there's *always* something new to learn. Michelangelo said *"The greatest danger for all of us lies not in setting our aim too high and falling short, but in setting our aim too low and achieving our mark."*

So, find the unrealized potential in people and make yourself determined to unleash it. When you convey to employees that *you* believe they have much more potential to grow, you'll be amazed by how much more they actually can become and contribute. Stretch people, set more challenging goals, and push all their perceived limits. Teach them new skills so they can strengthen their competency and become supremely self-confident. Never forget that when people feel capable, they execute fearlessly. *It's the role of leadership to draw out the greatest degree of effectiveness in people – for the employee's benefit – and for the benefit of the leader's own enterprise.*

It Builds Bench Strength For Your Team And Organization

It's only as we develop others that we permanently succeed.
Harvey Firestone

Nothing builds loyalty more than when employees feel you helped them progress in their lives. Developing people builds strong advocates when people realize you were the one who guided them, took a personal interest in them and invested in their becoming more.

But the leader also benefits when employees are fully trained and skilled to take on bigger roles before an opening exists. This proactive kind of development will not only elevate an employee's current performance but also helps you build a bench so you will always have talented and experienced people (people you already know and trust) filling your openings. The best benefit of all is that you never lose momentum when someone leaves. Leaders who are oriented to promote people from their own teams into higher levels of responsibility also tend to be the beneficiary of exceptional employee productivity. This is because people will work extremely hard when they see their doing so it likely to be rewarded. It fosters tremendous commitment.

Sometimes, leaders feel reluctant to help people grow – out of a fear that they'll end up losing someone who is highly productive and seemingly irreplaceable. I've been there. But I've learned a healthier, more realistic and more productive belief system: *Don't fight the natural order. Assume everyone will leave at some point. Allow people to move and make their own path.* The benefits of this approach are enormous. The surest way of losing people is to repress their growth. People can *feel* when their ambitions are being constricted. Always remember, it's through giving that we receive. By supporting people to achieve their career goals (even if that means they move somewhere else in the organization), you build a reputation for growing talent. And based upon this strong standing, new people will want to join your team.

Author, John C. Maxwell, said that there is a "Law of Magnetism" in leadership: Who you are as a leader is who you will attract. Said another way, by your helping others to grow, you're assured of attracting more people who want to achieve, excel and progress in their lives. These people are amazingly engaged and productive and they will flock to you. Just by helping people to grow, you very naturally will become a talent magnet! It also deserves mention that a reputation for successfully developing people is very likely to get you promoted as well.

The Windsor Knot Part II

On the night my father taught me to tie a Windsor knot, he displayed entirely uncharacteristic behavior. Ordinarily unsupportive and indifferent, he not only took the time to teach me to fully master a new skill, he thoughtfully passed on personal information and experience to further enrich my understanding. I remember how powerful and self-assured I felt after being so effectively trained. I so appreciated hearing my father's insights about the Windsor knot's decline in stylishness and being shown to make a dimple.

While my father is no model for effective leadership, there were things he did with me that evening which *were* enormously effective. Many years later, when I began leading people and was seeking ways of helping them master new skills and information, I recalled how I was taught the Windsor knot. As an adult, I saw that there were three steps my father had used to build my skill confidence. Not surprisingly, I adopted all three into my leadership practice, and have seen them have great effect on employee engagement and productivity. Specifically, my father taught me to *master the fundamentals*. He *shared his unique expertise.* He *coached me to win.*

Master The Fundamentals

> *You put good fundamentals on a player, you get a good player. You put great fundamentals on a player, you get a great player*[2].
>
> John Wooden

John Wooden, former head coach of the UCLA men's basketball team, is one of the greatest coaches – in any sport – in American history. Consider some of his achievements:

- He won 10 national championships. Seven of these came in successive years (1967-1973).
- In a still unprecedented fete, his teams won 88 games in a row – over several seasons and with different players.
- In a 29 year career, he won 80% of all games he coached.

Nearly forty years later, Wooden's run of dominance remains unmatched.

What made Wooden's teams so incredibly successful? His players were tremendously prepared and taught to master the fundamentals. Wooden's discipline was so great he took the time to teach his players how to put on their socks; he wanted to ensure wrinkled folds and creases didn't create blisters or other distractions during practice or in game time.

---

2   *Quotable John Wooden* by John Reger

If we want our employees to execute their jobs with tremendous confidence, we need to teach people so thoroughly that they learn the fundamentals by heart. Wooden once said "I would prefer to have my teams overconfident than with a lack of confidence. It's easier to bring a team down to reality that to give it confidence." Amen. Relentless competency building makes people assured so they can perform their roles in a superlative way. With that degree of inner knowing, people excel.

Here are two tricks I learned to ensure – once people are given job-based training – that they master the information and use the new knowledge to become masterful in their performance:

1. Test People

We think tests are only for college students, but I've learned testing people helps them really learn. People who have worked for me over the years are likely to describe my testing them as one of my more annoying – and stress producing – traits. No matter. They've all come to understand how much more proficient and successful they became in the process. Very recent research has proved that test taking cements knowledge better and helps people retain information for the long term so they can use it and implement it. Testing people holds them accountable. Essentially you're asking your employees to demonstrate that they understand.

I've used written tests and quizzes – perfect when introducing new products or methodologies – and routinely required that people demonstrate their skills by selling me a product or thoroughly performing a new process. There were many times when people didn't pass these tests. Not only were they required to re-test until they did pass, they were not allowed to discuss the new product with customers or perform a new procedure until they did. Testing raises your expectations of people and helps you certify employee proficiency.

2.   Teach People Advanced Skills

John Wooden's success as a leader owes much to his philosophy that a coach's job is to do more for players than just teach them basketball: *"If I could build the ideal coach, I would start with someone who was truly interested in those under his supervision in reasons other than their athletic ability."* In our context, develop the whole person; don't just teach them to do the task at hand.

We're too narrow in our thinking when we only train people to do the job they're assigned. I've learned people perform infinitely better – and teams perform far more effectively – when employees are challenged to learn some of the skills required in higher-level roles. Here's an example of how this led to an amazing success:

A bank where I had been a regional manager was acquired by a larger organization – a prominent home lender that sold home equity loan products never offered in our old bank. As soon as the acquisition was complete, it was expected that all the newly acquired branches be able to offer these products. This meant that people in these branches needed to be trained. The suggested strategy (made by our acquirer) was to start by training one person in each branch. Having one person trained in every branch, they argued, offered two benefits. First, it allowed all branches to begin selling the products and, second, the person trained could then help others on the team as they underwent training.

For me, there was no compelling logic in training just one person. (Who could speak to customers about the products when that one person was on break, or off from work that day, or on vacation?) While inherently far more ambitious, I decided to train *all* the sales employees at once. To help build really strong competency, I asked employees who had previous experience with the products to facilitate additional workshops. Once this process was underway, I did something no one else did – I selected several experienced tellers (a role which traditionally has no involvement in discussing or selling loan products) and trained them too. In just a few months, I had a huge percentage of my employees capable of handling customer inquiries, accepting applications and processing them to completion.

With our unusual competency in place, we learned that the most important goal for the next year (and several more years to come in turned out) would be home equity loan sales. This also meant that the richest financial rewards would go to all employees who had mastered the products and could drive business for the firm. Because we had so much depth of knowledge, and because we stretched a lot of people to do and learn more than was "normally" expected, my region set production records month after month. It wasn't very long before we were outperforming the more experienced regions of our acquirer. Because we operated out of an entirely different paradigm, many other regions didn't catch up with our exceptional productivity for over two years.

Even more satisfying to me was the example we set by raising the bar on our tellers. By training them to do more than their normal job, they felt honored. But they also made a huge contribution to our incomparable performance. Rather than forward customer calls to others in the branch, they were capable of answering questions on the spot and to providing customers far better service. This made the tellers feel terrific about themselves and their abilities, and helped them earn more. While some tellers later chose to move into sales positions, many remained in their original roles – feeling immensely more capable and self assured.

Share Your Expertise

After reading a really great book about leadership[3], I had the idea that it would be worthwhile for all my direct reports – bank managers at that time– to also read it. The next time I had my team together, I excitedly told them how insightful I thought the book was and offered them this sincere proposal:

"How about we all read the book and then devote time at our future meetings to discussing the chapters?"

3   *The Leadership Challenge,* by James Kouzes and Barry Posner

In quickly declining my offer, here's what they heard me say:

"How about we all read the book and then you will be <u>tested</u> on everything you read?"

While the managers didn't want to be tested on anything they perceived to be voluntary, they very cleverly suggested I take my offer to the assistant managers (their direct reports) and see if they might be more interested. I sensed a little bravado – as if my managers thought *they* were beyond the need to grow in their knowledge and skills but thought the assistant managers could use the help. Thinking my direct reports were missing out on a great opportunity, I decided it would be just as valuable for the next-level-down managers to acquire the information, so I went out and bought the books.

At the time, I was already conducting "job family" meetings and had been in the practice of bringing my most experienced[4] assistant managers together once a month for half-day sessions. Typically, these had been "dog and pony show" kinds of meetings where people from different departments in the organization (e.g. audit, operations, marketing) would come and present their updates. My normal role was to kick off the meeting and then turn things over to the presenters.

The next time the assistants were all together, I told them that I had plans to change things up in their meetings. I explained that we would have fewer outside speakers going forward so that we could spend more time focused on their leadership development – and on invaluable information not normally discussed in their day-to-day working positions. As I handed them each their new books, I asked them to read the first two chapters and to be ready to discuss the material in our next meeting.

Over the next month, I re-read the two chapters and made sure I fully understood the content in order to effectively lead the team's review. I also took time to compile a list of the book's most important ideas – the

---

4   Less experienced Assistant Managers had separate meetings.

information I most wanted the assistants to learn – and made it my goal to solicit their insights on each of them. During our discussions, once my employees had weighed in on a particular point, I made sure to validate their conclusions and to punctuate them by sharing experiences I'd had in my career where the same ideas applied.

To be true to myself, when we were through discussing the two chapters, I lined them all up against the wall (as if in a spelling bee) and asked them rapid-fire questions on the material. A wrong answer sent the employee back to their chair and a correct answer kept them in the game. Quite honestly, I was surprised. The assistants knew the material cold and the quiz lasted much longer than I expected. Witnessing their performance, I was excited by how much they knew and what that meant about their commitment to reading and learning.

We took four meetings to complete our review of the book but, every month, I noticed a transformation occurring. The assistants started to behave differently, carry themselves more maturely, dress more carefully and professionally – and perform at a higher level. I could see these people sprouting and growing right in front of me and gave all the credit to the book.

Encouraged by the success of our first venture, we started on another. Over the successive months, we read *The 7 Habits of Highly Effective People,*[5] *The 21 Irrefutable Laws of Leadership*[6], and *Emotional Intelligence*[7]. These three books are exceptional and we reviewed them in the same detail as we did the first book. It was unmistakable that the assistants were being transformed (several left the team by being promoted) and I was grateful I had chosen such life-changing material to review.

In an admittedly untraditional move, I devoted a few meetings to watching movies. We saw *Apollo 13, Braveheart, and the Gathering Storm* (a phenomenal film about Winston Churchill's extraordinary leadership

---

5   Author, Stephen Covey
6   Author, John C. Maxwell
7   Author, Daniel Goleman

in World War II) and distilled the stories down to their relationship to leadership effectiveness. At this point in our process, I reminded my employees that we had a business to run and that I needed them to come through for me if we were to continue to spend part of our business day this way. In some respects, I regret ever saying that because, independently, they had come to understand that what we were doing was different. They knew what burden fell to them and gladly accepted it. I never mentioned it again – and our firm-wide leading performance only got better month after month[8].

Next came a speech contest. Every assistant had to give a five-minute presentation on leadership. Almost no one was excited by the idea of speaking in front of me and their peers, and some gave themselves stomach aches worrying about it. No matter. We did it anyway. I met with each of them individually for a dress rehearsal and gave them guidance on what was working and where they could improve. On the day of the speech, I let the team vote on the winners. With few exceptions, the speeches were moving and inspiring and demonstrated the assistant's ability to integrate all the knowledge they had acquired from all the books and films. I was stirred by what these people had thought to do and had executed so brilliantly.

At this point, the managers came back and "accused" me of neglecting their leadership development. They saw how their own subordinates had skyrocketed in capacity and self-confidence and wanted in. I reminded them that they were resistant at first (they knew) but promised I would do all the same things with them. At our very first meeting, when we reviewed the first two chapters of the *Leadership Challenge,* the managers were so incredibly engaged I was totally blown away. I saw their intense and pent up desire to grow – and their willingness to do the work to achieve it.

Even though I owe a debt of gratitude to all the authors and film directors whose work greatly educated my teams, I ultimately came to understand

---

8   In reality, our four-hour monthly meetings – in which leadership development was just one component – represented only 2% of the hours employees worked every month.

that it wasn't the books or the movies that had been so galvanizing to my employees– it was the fact that I, as their leader, was spending time with them and specifically sharing a lot of my own expertise in the process. People understood I was investing in them by giving of myself and sharing ideas and experiences they had yet to have.

As leaders, we too often underestimate how much knowledge and wisdom we have acquired – and how much good it can do to share it with people who work for us. I've learned that employees *love it* when leaders open up and purposely pass on their philosophy and perspective. Doing this not only reinforces employee's feeling of connection to you, it also gives them greater insight into you. With this more intimate understanding, you help them become more effective in implementing your intention. The lesson here is that personal contact with leaders tends to be quite inspiring to future performance.

Coach To Win

You'll remember the night I learned to tie a Windsor knot that my father put me through the paces – his process of teaching me was filled with high expectations and great rigor: he insisted I learn it, kept me up late, drilled me until I could literally tie it with my eyes closed which made me more skillful at the task than was ever required.

As a surprise to me, I never felt put upon or believed he was being too challenging or demanding. Instead, I could tell that he really cared about making me proficient and was doing all the things he believed would ensure I could excel. I sensed that my success mattered to him and that he was coaching me as best as he knew how – coaching me to win. Because of this, I *enthusiastically* responded to his greater requirements.

My tie-learning experience was the first to give me these two invaluable insights:

- *People will meet and often exceed the highest expectations and demands when they know their leader values and cares about them.*

- *It's only when leaders are able to set very high expectations, and to challenge people to do more, that teams ever achieve superlative results.*

Consider the example of Dick Vermiel, the only person ever to be named "Coach of the Year" while leading football teams at every competitive level: High School, Junior College, Collegiate Division I and the National Football League – where he earned the honor twice. He took two different teams to the Superbowl and led the St. Louis Rams to the championship in Superbowl XXIV.

Vermiel may be one of the most demanding sports team leaders ever. Adopting disciplines and a work ethic he learned from a father who owned a car repair shop and routinely worked eighteen hours a day, he pushed his players through three hour practices – often the longest in the league. Believing that winning always requires hard work and sacrifice, Vermiel was one tough boss. But his success throughout his career owes more to his heart than to the exhausting process he used to prepare his players. Vermiel "learned to treat and coach people as individuals." While he pressed players to master skills and execute flawlessly, he also showered them with appreciation and even compassion expressing once, "If you care, they'll care." And Vermiel wasn't afraid to show emotion. He gave impassioned locker room speeches, frequently hugged players, and publicly lauded their performance. Following emotional wins, he made no attempt to shield tears of joy.

None of this behavior ever hurt his team's performance. Instead, in the modern-day gladiator world of the National Football League, it only compelled his players to work with greater commitment and effort. Vermiel made it evident to players that he cared for them personally: "I've said it a million times that nobody has a better relationship with his players than I do." And players felt it and trusted it. Kansas City Chief's tight-end, Tony Gonzalez, once said of his former coach, "The way he opens his heart…you can tell it's genuine." Vermiel may have expected a lot from people, but by balancing the production orientation with individual concern and care, he motivated them to not only perform at consistently high levels – but to win.

Vermiel was also an extremely popular coach with the fans. The most hard-core football devotees could see the powerful connection he had with his players, how very hard they worked for him and how passionate he was about seeing his players succeed. Fans were *inspired* by this.

Vermiel, whose biography is appropriately titled, *"Whistle In His Mouth, Heart On His Sleeve,"* clearly understood that the heart is the core of people and of teams. By coaching in a far more human way, he was able to motivate his players to meet exceedingly high expectations and to do all that was necessary to perform to their highest capacity. It makes no sense, really, that we embrace the heart in sports leadership – where winning is everything and snub it in business leadership – where... winning is everything.

CHAPTER 8

INSPIRE THE HEART:
VALUE AND HONOR ACHIEVEMENTS

There is more hunger for love and appreciation in this world than for bread.

Mother Theresa

In January, 1991, HomeFed Bank – a then sixty-year-old financial institution – announced with great fanfare that its annual earnings were the firm's all-time best. Because the bank had been building momentum for several consecutive years, the news of record profits reinforced expectations that an even more prosperous future lay ahead. And so, it was both alarming and unexpected when HomeFed revealed just three months later that it was suffering a first quarter loss – in an amount so large it would wipe out all of the previous *years'* banner income.

When investors heard the news, the bank's stock price plummeted. Industry analysts were spooked by the surprise and raised concerns about management's ability to accurately assess the severity of its problems. Because the loss was so large and so sudden, they suggested much worse news may be in the offing. Overnight, HomeFed's survival had been put in question.

In the days following announcement, the executive management team dug into the financial analysis and weighed its options. Fearing the bank's situation was indeed dire, and wanting to preserve as much capital as possible, HomeFed's president directed his business heads to make severe expense reductions across the company.

I was a young leader at HomeFed at the time and these cuts would have an enormously disruptive impact on my area of responsibility. Never having faced a crisis like this, the challenges I was asked to manage initially seemed oppressive and unconquerable to me. But how we successfully maneuvered through these extraordinary circumstances gave me tremendous insight into the human spirit and what sustains it. In one of the most profoundly impactful experiences of my career, I learned how fundamentally important it is to acknowledge, value, and honor people for their contributions as a means of inspiring their greatest performance. More specifically, I learned that recognition – when given genuinely as an expression of gratitude – is the most powerful and essential leadership practice of all.

HomeFed Bank[1] was founded in the Great Depression and experienced its greatest growth and success in the years I worked there. As my first job after college, I joined the company as a management trainee in 1982, just as a punishing recession was ending and interest rates were falling precipitously from historic highs. Over the next several years, the firm exploited the greatly improved economy and became a dominant home lender and real estate developer. They also used their expanding wealth to build and acquire bank branches. By 1990, HomeFed had become the sixth largest savings bank[2] in the nation with over 200 branches in the then flourishing state of California.

HomeFed also was extremely innovative. They were one of the first banks in the country to install a comprehensive sales culture. Beginning in the mid-1980's, a visionary executive adopted the sales methods of successful retailers – a move later made by all U.S. banks. Upending a tradition of passive product selling, he made branch managers and their employees accountable for the achievement of ever increasing

---

1   Originally Home Federal Savings and Loan.
2   Also known as a "thrift."

sales targets, requiring them to be much more proactive in presenting the bank's products and services (e.g. loans, deposits, investments) to customers. To develop competency and self-confidence, he provided employees comprehensive sales training and coaching. With help from an external consultant, he re-architected all compensation plans by reducing salaries and introducing sales incentives and bonuses as rewards for goal achievement. It took a few years for employees to adapt to and embrace the new culture, but heading into the new decade, HomeFed's retail banking productivity had earned industry-wide acclaim. Branch employees also found themselves earning more money than ever. Tied to their ever-improving effectiveness in driving sales, they were earning a quarter or more of their total income from sales incentives.

Just a few months before the loss announcement, and with the new "sales program" up and running, I was put in charge of sales management for retail banking. Essentially, it became my job to advance the bank's sales effectiveness and to ensure all HomeFed branches became more productive and profitable. I became responsible for designing all of the branch incentive plans, sales campaigns and recognition efforts. At the time, the company relied heavily on financial rewards to drive performance. While it recognized exceptional employee achievement, it did so formally just once each year.

As a means of diversifying its income, HomeFed ventured into commercial lending – an area where it previously had little expertise. The first quarter loss was entirely the result of very large commercial loans which had been placed into foreclosure. None of the losses had anything to do with retail banking. In fact, at the time of the loss, the branch network was excelling against their goals and driving substantial revenue for the firm.

Even though the branch network had not contributed to the bank's problems, like all other divisions in the firm, we were told to brace for cuts. I likely was in denial at the time (or not yet fully understanding the severity of HomeFed's condition) and had convinced myself that expense reductions imposed upon us would be superficial. I completely understood that everyone should be made to sacrifice in the interest of assuring the company's future existence – but I wasn't expecting anything too drastic. Consequently, I was entirely unprepared for the decision which came down:

All branch manager incentives were suspended (i.e. terminated indefinitely) and all other branch employee incentives were radically reduced.

When I heard the news, fear-based adrenaline shot through my system along with a rapid-fire list of concerns. I imagined the wholesale departure of managers and their employees (who would stick around when there now was little financial motivation to do so?). I foresaw competitors exploiting the opportunity and aggressively recruiting against us. I envisioned an entirely de-motivated work force just at the time when we needed the highest degree of commitment, enthusiasm and emotional presence.

Something else was circulating around my psyche in that moment. Believing that money was the most important driver of sales performance, I had no instinctive answer to how I could keep employees engaged. A day later, I still had no idea what to do – a situation made worse when my boss challenged me to "quickly find creative ways of sustaining our productivity."

Without any compelling answers of my own, I made a call to the consultant the bank used when laying down the foundation for the sales culture. I desperately explained our company's reversal of fortune and asked if he could come up with any ideas to help me. After hearing my plight, he very calmly and confidently gave me this guidance: *"Mark, you're just going to have to leverage recognition."*

Just hearing I might have a solution – Plan B – heartened me even though he offered no details on how to implement the idea and make it effective. But perhaps because of my own upbringing (and greater sensitivity to the effects of feeling valued), I realized he was on to something. The thought running through my mind was "If *I* was a branch employee being asked to perform – and perform well - in the absence of financial incentives, what would *I* want?" And the answer came immediately. If I was to forego substantial financial rewards (i.e. income) for the purpose of helping the bank survive, I would at least want to know all my hard work and sacrifice was appreciated. *"Tell me you understand and that you are grateful."*

This insight led me to develop a quarterly, bank-wide recognition program.

For the purpose of symbolically linking the company's past triumphs over difficult times and challenges, we named our program – and a new award – in honor of HomeFed's founder, Charles K. Fletcher. In a letter sent to every bank employee, HomeFed's Chairman expressed the company's regret that sales incentives had been suspended along with a reiteration of how important everyone's effort and commitment would be over the coming weeks and months.

He told employees that their sacrifice would not be taken for granted and that a new award had been created specifically to acknowledge their highest achievements. He very proudly announced that HomeFed's new award, the Charles K. Fletcher Award of Excellence, had special meaning and importance to him; it bore the name of his father.

While we had very little money to spend, we promised employees that executive managers would host quarterly recognition awards ceremonies[3] to formally and personally acknowledge the most outstanding performances made by branch teams and by individual employees. We were clear in stating that there was no corresponding monetary component to the award and that recipients would receive a congratulatory letter signed by the Retail Banking President along with a small award memento. That's all.

Days and even weeks after employees read the Chairman's letter, newspaper and television coverage of HomeFed's perilous condition

---

3   Held in the evening and across the state so all branch employees could attend.

persisted, making the branch environment particularly stressful. Employees exhausted a lot of energy assuaging customer fears and often were distracted away from their now-more-difficult efforts at driving incremental sales performance. Since we were living according to an entirely new world order, we really had no way of knowing how the branches – and, more specifically how the *people* – would perform over the next period of months and whether spirits would inevitably be defeated.

In the early going, neither turnover nor sales performance deteriorated significantly. We thought this exceptional at the time, and quite encouraging under the circumstances. But we also understood it would take time to determine how employees truly were responding. In three months or so, we would hold our first CKF Awards events. Knowing attendance at these was voluntary, we all believed turnout for these would be the best gauge of our employee's continuing engagement.

We held our very first event on a warm summer evening in a company cafeteria. Executives arrived early and helped blow up balloons and bring out chairs. We set up a modest stage, tested the microphones, straightened our ties and reviewed the agenda. No one had any idea whether this assembly would be meaningful enough for people to want to come. Knowing what was at stake, I felt quite uneasy. The cafeteria crew put hotdogs and hamburgers on the grill just as the branches all were closing their doors. We had everything ready and waited anxiously to see if employees would arrive.

Making their way from nearly 60 different locations, *they came*. And they didn't come out of a sense of obligation – they came *enthusiastically*. Many wore tee-shirts and hats they had made especially for this occasion – paying for them out of their own pockets. People walked in carrying signs and painted banners. Before we ever began the event, employees quickly turned it into their own pep rally – for themselves and for the future of HomeFed. As the emcee for the awards ceremony, I was preempted by several employees who had prepared skits and even songs for the occasion. By the time I came on stage and launched the meeting officially, everyone in the room was standing up, screaming cheers and wildly clapping their hands. It was simply wonderful.

Our senior executives spoke one after another. Unscripted – and clearly speaking from their hearts – they expressed their gratitude for all that people had been asked to deal with. They acknowledged how overwhelmed people were feeling and told story after story about employees doing heroic things for the company. Remarkably, sales performance in the branches barely suffered in that first quarter and everyone in the room was appropriately and collectively acknowledged.

When CKF Award winners[4] came on stage, they were hugged, had their hands shaken and received hearty pats on their backs by all their leaders. What I will always remember from this first event – and from all the others that followed – was the supreme joy employees displayed when their names were called. Some *ran* up on stage, some cried and others beamed. They knew how hard they had worked and how much of themselves they had given. But what made it all worthwhile to them was that the recognition was sincere and they could *feel* it. They knew all they had done truly mattered.[5]

Over the next five quarters, the vast majority of HomeFed's employees chose to stay with the company all the while remaining extremely hard working and committed to helping it endure. Amazingly, engagement stayed high all through that time.[6] Ultimately, the commercial loan cancer outstripped the vitality of the retail bank and HomeFed failed in July, 1992. Sadly, had HomeFed's fate been solely tied to the performance of its retail branches, its demise might have been averted.

---

4   The top 25% performers along with others receiving special recognition.

5   Throughout those events I had countless employees thank *me* for making *them* feel so appreciated.

6   It wasn't recognition alone that got so many employees to stay. Many had worked for the bank for many years and were vested in its future were it to have succeeded. But engagement and productivity stayed high during desperate times because people were made to feel all they were doing was valued throughout the firm.

It was, of course, devastating to all of us who worked there to see the bank fail and later be sold off. But, in one very important sense, I'm grateful for having had the experience of my last year there specific to our implementation of a formal and consistent recognition process. It taught me an invaluable lesson on leadership effectiveness that served me well for years to come.

At the time we launched the CKF Award, I had an instinctive and very personal sense that it would be very meaningful to employees to know and feel they were appreciated as they worked through disconcerting times and challenges. But what the experience taught me is that being acknowledged for what one does and achieves is a fundamental *human* need that should never be consigned to just the most trying circumstances. *Feeling valued is essential to the well being of all people and to the spirit which motivates performance.*

Few things have as powerful effect on any of us than hearing our boss tell us that they are proud of us. That our work is really good. This is because we all need to know that our contributions count for something – that we are helping the leader and our organization succeed. Leaders too often disregard how critically important this is to people, how it inspires and why it's so essential to sustaining high performance.

Unlike pay and other financial rewards, being praised and recognized is an expression of care, and this – and not money – affects the hearts in people. If we want to see specific behaviors repeated, we must be consistently swift in praising it. By focusing on what is working well, we inherently invite more of the same. This is because people naturally *want to do* all that is valued and acknowledged.

It's been my consistent experience that many leaders (and even companies) don't celebrate their achievements at all. Following a successful month, quarter, or campaign, they immediately focus on the next goal, the next challenge and completely ignore the hard work and tremendous effort made by their subordinates. And so they plow forward without any moment taken to acknowledge all the commitment and achievement.

Employees are given no time to catch their breath, savor the moment or feel a sense of satisfaction with what they just accomplished. Leading this way is just enormously destructive to future effort. *If you want to kill the goose that laid the golden egg, this is the way to do it.*

Bruce Cryer provides another compelling reason for why recognition is so important to effective leadership: "The art of stopping to appreciate actually is a tremendous source of renewal [for people] and helps widen their perspective about the achievability of whatever challenges they still have to face." "Challenges ahead become more manageable and doable because they have the immediate perspective of accomplishing something – and knowing it was appreciated."

Following my experience with HomeFed and the CKF Award program, my sense of awe for the power of recognition only grew greater. Seeking to make my recognition of people drive the greatest engagement and productivity, I experimented with different approaches and practices. After twenty more years of testing and observing, I concluded there are five habits leaders must develop in order to maximize the effect of recognition and thereby derive its greatest benefits;

1. Give Recognition Only When Its Earned

In 2009, author, Bruce Tulgan, wrote a cleverly titled book, "Not Everybody Gets A Trophy," as a guide for managing Gen-Y workers (born 1978-1991) who as children quite often were awarded trophies just for *participating* in activities like soccer and little league baseball. The idea of handing trophies to everyone, and not just to kids whose teams win a championship, came out of a belief that it would build self-esteem. It's since been found to be completely misguided. And it's just as bad an idea – even out of a generous spirit – to give working adults recognition when it's not deserved.

Employees must understand what standard of performance a leader expects and also to know that meeting these standards will be met with praise. The meaning and importance of recognition to people is fully diluted when it's not fully earned. Much like the teacher who hands out "A's" to every student, the grade rings hollow for the students who know they didn't really earn it. Even worse, it suggests to those who did that their extra effort wasn't really worth it – and won't be worth it in the future. The leader's job is to hold people to high standards, proactively help them reach them and to authentically honor those whose achievements warrant it.

2. Never Ration Recognition When It *Is* Earned

We've somehow been led to believe that rationing recognition or extending it to just a few people, the top 3, for example, is logical. This idea must be rejected. Your objective as a leader is to make *every* person on your team effective. To not honor and acknowledge achievement that meets or exceeds the very targets you set for people is the surest way of defeating an employee's spirit, initiative and drive.

Some leaders may have it in their minds that recognizing employees more routinely has the greater potential of dimishing performance – that too much praising and thanking employees will deaden ambitions as pre-meal cookies spoils children's appetites. This is simply not the case. Here's what I have learned.

Unless the leader takes things to saccharine excess, it's almost impossible to over appreciate people. As long as praise is earned and deserved, acknowledging performance only has the effect of inspiring greater future effort and commitment. *Not* praising it is clearly harmful and ignoring accomplishment in the belief that it's an example of someone "just doing their job" is leadership malpractice. Reserving recognition just for unique or long-term achievements also undermines people and their performance.

More people will achieve their long-term targets when they are acknowledged for accomplishing the intermittent ones. It's also interesting that when people are infrequently praised, an unnatural competition between co-workers develops. This is because people come to believe they must out-do each other in order to win the leader's approval — the few times he or she provides it. For teams to thrive, people must work well together. A scarcity of praise leads people to hoard ideas, demonstrate less cooperation, and otherwise do things in their own self interests. When praise is abundant, people are generous and supportive of one another. People are happy when others are recognized and confident their hard work will be acknowledged as well.

3. Ensure All Recognition Is Genuine And Sincere

What comes from the heart, goes to the heart.
Samuel Taylor Coleridge

The idea that recognition is important seems to be widely accepted in business but what too often gets missed is the spirit behind the practice. People can sense when a leader is expressing real appreciation, and only when it's genuine can it deeply affect people. Conversely, when it doesn't come sincerely — from the heart — the recognition has little chance of affecting someone else.

I can't count the number of times I received some kind of acknowledgement when the leader was simply going through the motions — methodically calling off names from a list, intent upon getting through the exercise and to move on to more important things. In these instances, I knew it *was* recognition, but because I could tell the person acknowledging me wasn't really present and wasn't connecting to any authentic feelings of appreciation, the recognition had little of its intended effect. On these occasions I often left feeling *un*appreciated. As a result, insincere, disingenuous recognition can be more harmful than giving no recognition at all.

Recognition is an act of giving and of reinforcing the value and contributions of people. Through your words, your intonation and physiology, make it apparent that you are thriving in your employee's success, honored by their effort and that their high achievements matter to you personally. As a reminder, this doesn't call on a leader to gush or over do the praise. If you truly value people and the accomplishments they make, the right behavior can be expected to flow naturally.

4. Institutionalize Recognition

It was an epiphany for me when I first realized people will work really hard to earn recognition.

At one of my team meetings, I congratulated several employees who had performed exceptionally well the previous month. I announced their results, called them up one-by-one and presented them with a certificate and a small box of candy. When the meeting was over, a new employee who had not been recognized looked back at me as she was leaving the room and shouted, "You'll be calling out my name next month!"

In the moment, I thought that her remark was really cool. She was telling me to expect her to excel over the next thirty days – she planned to bring it on! But it was later that I also understood she was conveying her own expectations. As the reward for her great results a month from now, she fully expected to receive the exact same kind of recognition she just saw her teammates receive.

My initial insight was that this employee was motivated to accomplish great things just in order to be recognized. But it also meant that she would be extremely disappointed were I to not make good on my end. We were all taught to provide intermittent rewards to people as a means of reinforcing desired behaviors. But when it comes to the workplace, when people are willing to kill themselves just to be acknowledged, it's simply destructive to not provide recognition when its been earned.

Once I fully understood this, I decided I must institutionalize recognition – meaning that I needed to inform my team what specific performance I would consistently recognize and then deliver upon that promise without fail. I laid out our goals, emphasized which ones were most important and then created a designated time throughout the year to acknowledge collective and individual achievements. I wanted to make sure everyone who worked for me came to *expect* that high performance and achievement would be consistently rewarded – to *know* their great work would *always* be honored.

Provide Monthly Recognition

While it's typical for leaders to review and discuss their enterprise's results over much shorter intervals, a reasonably long period of performance is required for *formal* recognition to be appropriate or meaningful.[7] Consequently, I learned the ideal time to honor team achievements is at the start of every month, at a team meeting where all members are present.

It's also very logical to lead off these meetings with recognition. You need to take time to review and assess – and acknowledge – the most recent performance before you effectively have the right to ask your team to take on any new challenges. In other words, you must show your appreciation for successes and progress made before you can appropriately direct the team to whatever comes next – to whatever you will be asking them to accomplish right after they leave your meeting.

Recognition As Ritual

At the beginning of every meeting, I distributed our key performance reporting, the team's results against our most important targets. To establish continuity and predictability, we reviewed the same reports, in the same order, for an entire year and acknowledged team and individual accomplishments in every category. By being this dependable, we inadvertently created a powerful ritual for our team. And rituals, it turns out, are really good for people. According to Paul Pearsall, research has shown that rituals have demonstrably positive effects on the heart and on the immune system. Rituals create the sense that valued elements of life's experiences are stable, predictable and enduring. And these

---

7   More informally acknowledging performance in the interim is, of course, necessary.

kinds of rituals bond teams together giving people essential feelings of connection.

Make Recognition A Ceremony – A Celebration

Call people to the front of the room. Have them stand. Clap for them. Make your recognition a ceremony. Take time to describe the hurdles people faced – tell the team what behaviors led a person to perform so well. Doing this doesn't just honor the person you are recognizing, it explains to everyone on the team what behaviors you value most.

Use A Consistent Token Of Appreciation

I stumbled across one of the most effective drivers of performance when I began giving away candy to employees being recognized at monthly meetings.

One month when my team of managers had a particularly great month, I bought small bags of candy[8] to use as a special reward. While reviewing our results, I tossed one of these bags to every manager whose branch met or exceeded goal in any of our key sales targets.

Because it was such a successful month, almost every manager went back to their offices with at least one bag of candy (many earned several) which had the initially unintended effect of extending the recognition to all of the employees working in the branch – the people who helped their managers achieve the goals. When employees understood why the candy had been brought back to the branch, they felt validated and were proud that I had noticed and honored their performance.

I never saw so many people get so excited over something they could buy for themselves for three dollars! That, of course, wasn't the point. The candy was a symbol of achievement – a spoil of success – that, once again, people proved extremely willing to work for. This will seem

---

8   Small bags of miniature Milky Ways, Mounds bars, Snickers et al commonly found in grocery stores.

like a crazy connection to some, but when I introduced the candy, then continued the practice ever after, my region of 25 branches led the nation-wide company (85 regions) for the next three consecutive *years*. (I recognized individual achievement with large boxes of Junior Mints).

Never varying the award (it was the same bags of candy and the same Junior Mints month after month) allowed our team to build a tradition. It gave people something to look forward to each month – and to work for –and further reinforced the team's rituals. We used candy as a tangible acknowledgement of performance but any consistent token can be used to great effect.

5. Encourage People

Had it not been for some timely encouragement from his wife, the now prolific and enormously successful writer, Stephen King, may never have written his first book – or, consequently, any of the others he's gone on to produce. While writing what later would become the best seller, *Carrie,* King was working two jobs and struggling to make ends meet. Not yet fully confident in the quality or marketability of his writing and discouraged by having no money to fix his car or even get a phone, he threw the first draft of his book in the garbage.

Fortunately for all of his many readers and fans, Kings' wife later pulled the pages out of the trash pail, "shook the cigarette ashes off the crumpled balls of paper, smoothed them out and sat down to read them."[9] And when she was done, she redirected the trajectory of her husband's life telling him directly, "I think you've got something here. I really do."

In his book, *On Writing, A Memoir of the Craft,* King recalled the significance of that moment and how his wife's thoughtful actions and encouraging words as he wrote inspired him to finish his first book:

---

9   Stephen King, *"On Writing, A Memoir of the Craft"*

"My wife made a crucial difference during those two years I spent teaching at Hayden (and washing sheets at the New Franklin laundry during the summer vacation). If she had suggested that the time I spent writing stories on the front porch of our rented house on Pond Street or in the laundry of our rented trailer on Klatt Road in Hermon was a waste of time, I think a lot of heart would have gone out of me." "Writing is a lonely job. Having someone who believes in you makes a lot of difference."

When I first gave thought to writing my own book, I had the fantasy of being able to sit down and type away with the speed of a court reporter. I honestly thought I'd be able to make fast work of it. But as I faced my first blank screen and began to more fully understand all I had signed up for, there were more days than not when I wondered if I could do this – whether, at some point, I would have to disclose that the project vanquished me – that it proved beyond my capabilities. Even though I know it's my nature to be willful and persistent and that these traits generally assure I complete things I take on, I sincerely believe my having finished this book had much to do with people in my life who very thoughtfully chose to encourage me along the way.

This is not hyperbole. Words that expressed belief in me and my ability to succeed had an enormously beneficial effect when the task at hand seemed too big and imposing. In writing my first book, I was out of my comfort zone, and supportive words from friends and family heartened me to go on – to make it a productive day and to stay the course.

I'm not the only one on the planet to ever doubt his abilities or to be fearful when faced with big challenges. These feelings are *universal*. More specifically, people go to work every day worried that they won't be able to meet their leader's expectations. Even worse, people impose deeply self-limiting beliefs upon themselves and upon their own potential. These fears of inadequacy unnecessarily restrict people from attempting bigger challenges, demonstrating initiative or growing in levels of responsibility.

The power of encouragement, as an antidote to doubt and fear, is inestimable. Giving people encouragement when they are struggling, worried they can't measure up or faced with a new wall to climb is the tonic which helps people exceed their own expectations. Encouragement inspires optimism and influences people to become and accomplish more.

The word "encourage" dates back to the fourteenth century and, not surprisingly, means "to give heart" to people. Encourage means to reassure and embolden. Encouragement inspires people to try new approaches and to persist in the face of a daunting task. Words and actions of encouragement breathe life into the hopes and dreams of people, and express the leader's belief that they have the power to accomplish whatever they desire or have in front of them. Employees are attentive to everything a leader says and does and words and gestures of encouragement are long remembered – especially in moments when work seems most difficult.

American poet, Archibald Macleish, insightfully conveyed the power of encouragement by advising us to "blow on the coal of the heart." So tell people directly – in your own words or in any of these:

- *I believe in you.*
- *I know you can accomplish this. I'm certain of it.*
- *We'll celebrate when you achieve it!*
- *I see how much potential you have and know only great things lay ahead for you.*
- *You may doubt yourself, but I have no doubt in you.*
- *You sooooo can do this!*

There are many ways to accomplish this. Send an e-mail to the entire team to express your confidence in them. Handwrite a note to someone you want to more personally support. (Doing this is extremely meaningful to people. Many former employees of mine have told me they still have notes I sent them years after we worked together). Express it to people in meetings, when you are coaching – whenever you sense someone needs it. By encouraging employees, you positively affect their hearts and thereby inspire greater performance.

CONCLUSION

What we do in life echoes in eternity.
Maximus Decimus Meridias
Roman General, 152-192 A.D.

To announce my selection as a regional manager, my new organization sent out a very complimentary communication which conveyed my background and career experience. It was well known in the company that several people had been considered for the role and the announcement expressed that I had been the most qualified candidate and had a reputation for being a very thoughtful leader. With the skids greased so nicely for me, I went into my first meeting with my new team of managers ecstatic about the opportunity and anticipating a gracious welcome.

I didn't get one. Almost from the minute I walked into the room, I was met by deliberate coldness. Some of the people on my new team were outright hostile and it just stunned me. I spent the entire meeting wondering what I could have done to put off people so severely that they felt very comfortable interrupting me while I was speaking and directly challenging things I was saying. Not everyone was so overtly resistant, but a handful of my employees clearly wanted me to know they didn't think I had been the right choice for the job.

My experience that day had a truly bizarre explanation. One of my new direct reports, Janie, had gone out of her way to rile up her peers by alleging that I was a micro-manager of the worst kind. She induced the worst kind of fear by suggesting I would be holding frequent conference calls, pushing people to meet excessively high goals, and punishing them when they were unsuccessful. She insisted I would quickly take away their autonomy and urged them all to collectively reject me so that I would be forced to leave.

Janie based all these expectations of me on a hallucination. I had no history of ever leading people as she had described – but someone else in her past had. Marty, a regional manager Janie once worked for, had indeed managed this way. Janie was someone who thrived on independence and the satisfaction of achieving success through her own leadership. It simply killed her spirit to have her work-life so tightly controlled. She had withered under Marty's leadership and was determined to never again work for someone who managed this way.

What was entirely lost on Janie was that *I* wasn't Marty. What Janie knew to be true was that I had come from the same organization where Marty was now working. She also knew Marty had been allowed to continue his repressive ways at that company. Based on these two facts alone, Janie made the grand – and illogical – assumption that Marty was back; this time incarnated in a different body and with a different name.

It took me a few months to understand that Janie's weird fantasy had made so many on my team want to do me in. And it was several months after that when my still-new boss told me that Janie had sent a letter to the president of the bank – signed by several others on my team – directly stating that they had made a horrible error in hiring me and requesting that I be immediately replaced. I was mortified that Janie would do such a thing and was very concerned that I had gotten off to a rocky start with my new employer. This was my career after all.

While I probably had every reason to retaliate – Janie continued for several months to fight me on things I wanted to do in the region often insisting that I follow her advice on my execution – I decided to take a different tack. First of all, I knew I wasn't a micro-manager. Second,

I knew how I had led people in the past resulted in me having very good relationships with my employees. Rather than panic, I decided to follow my own normal program and demonstrate to Janie that her fears were unfounded.

I began by trying to build a personal relationship with her. I was by no means successful in winning her over in our first discussion, but I specifically made a point of acknowledging her for the things I knew mattered to her – her work ethic, her solid relationship with her customers and employees, and her ability to perform without constant direction. I also offered her coaching in some areas where she was less experienced. She refused the help, of course, but I ended our meeting feeling as if some of the ice was thawing.

Where I first saw a change in Janie was during our recognition sessions. She always worked very hard and consistently performed well. As a result, she frequently was applauded for her team's achievements. I knew early on that being appreciated mattered greatly to her. But I also noticed she delighted when others on the team were recognized. She clearly enjoyed being a part of a winning team. There was no immediate transformation – it took me well over a year before our relationship became less confrontational – but, inevitably, Janie became a supporter. Seeing people she had worked with for years now performing at exceedingly higher levels, she gave me the credit. She started advocating for me with the rest of my managers seeking to assure them that I really had their best interests at heart. None of this lasted very long, however. Unfortunately, Janie was diagnosed with cancer and was forced to take a leave of absence.

To support the branch in her absence, I brought in an experienced assistant manager and implored the entire team to do their very best over the coming months – to make Janie proud. Continuing to treat her as an active member of my team, I faxed reports to her house so she could see how her branch and the region were performing. To keep her spirits high, I sent get-well cards from our team along with bags of candy her employees had earned. I paid close attention to her branch in hopes that it would be hitting on all cylinders when she returned. Janie progressed through surgery, chemotherapy, hair loss and a long recovery before finally returning to her branch. I was there to welcome her back. Just a few months later, Janie went out on leave again and, soon after, succumbed to the cancer. We never really got to enjoy the relationship we could have had, but I was certainly grateful we had made the relationship harmonious before her death.

A couple of days after Janie died, her daughter called me and told me that her mother had asked if I would speak at her funeral. Janie's posthumous gesture touched me deeply and it most certainly wasn't lost on me how far our relationship had come. Knowing Janie would have appreciated me speaking the truth, I prepared a eulogy which retold the story of our relationship: how she had been determined to run my region, how she had written the letter to the president, and how I came to be speaking at her memorial. I had great enjoyment preparing these remarks knowing that I would be using them to eulogize someone who had become a dear friend.

Just before the service was to begin, the church pastor came into the anteroom and introduced himself. He pointed to where he wanted me to sit and explained when I would come up to speak. Our conversation was cordial and brief. Seconds later, as we were walking together toward the large congregation, he leaned over to me and said, "You better be good."

Better be good? I thought this was a particularly odd thing for a cleric to be saying to me under the circumstances and so I whispered back "What do you mean?" Leaning into me again, and putting his arm on my shoulder, he said "You know Janie wanted you to be the *only* speaker, don't you?"

Over all the past 25 years I have led people, I was a fierce competitor. In any given week, month or year, I was extremely focused on achieving the goals in front of me and on seeing my teams excel. As I look back on all that time, I realize I only have a *broad* recollection of our accomplishments. I know we performed exceptionally well, set records and won awards. But what I don't remember with any specificity were the actual results. I can't recall how much investment revenue we produced in any given month or even the sales results which toppled a twenty-five year company record.

Here's what I have come to realize. Long after you can remember the actual work or the targets you met along the way, what's sustained in your memory is the effect you had on people's *lives*. By this one measure, above all others, you'll know the true impact you had as a leader.

AN INVITATION FROM MARK C. CROWLEY: JOIN MY TRIBE!

Thank you for reading this book!

Please join the growing tribe of people who believe that leading from the heart is the most effective and sustainable way of inspiring human achievement in the workplace.

Our website is www.markccrowley.com, where you'll find updated ideas, advice and stories, as well as links to conversations with like-minded leaders from all over the country.

I hope you'll join me in the movement to positively change the way we lead!

ACKNOWLEDGMENTS

This book has been greatly enriched by insights provided by Bruce Cryer, Alex Edmans, John Gibbons and Dr. Mimi Guaneri. I am deeply grateful to each of them for believing in my thesis and for so generously sharing their uncommon knowledge. All four have left their personal signature in these pages.

Otherworldly guidance I received from Kerri Finnecy and Lisa Renee helped me come to fully trust my own voice and message. I'm profoundly thankful to you both.

Forty years after living next door to Carolyn Whitman, my appreciation for the wonderful woman who provided me a sanctuary and love as a young boy endures. Her recent recollections of my early-life experiences gave me new perspective and helped me to more fully understand how I was influenced to lead from the heart.

For good reason, I trusted my great friend, Scott Davis, to be the first reader of every chapter in the book. Early in the process, I discovered he had a talent for providing incisive literary direction and an inclination to hold my writing to very high standards. The reassurance he provided me during our weekly Sunday morning runs sustained my spirits all the way to completion.

After I'd outlined all of my proposed chapters, I relied on a small group of trusted and talented friends to guide me. Their feedback early on helped set the book in motion and informed my writing. My sincere thanks go to Cecilia Gudino, Dr. Rick Jensen, Don Elliott, Michael Lang, Keely Minton, Marci McWilliams, Doug Jackson and Phyllis Adamo.

I owe my editor, friend and confidante, Susan DeRoche, an enormous debt of gratitude for investing so much of her time and expertise into making my expression more clear, concise and direct. That she was moonlighting the entire time she worked on the project only makes me more appreciative.

Once the book was complete, I needed – and received – great support and guidance on how best to layout and design the book and its cover. For this generous help, I'm very, very grateful to Ken Boynton who is clever and talented beyond words.

It's been over twenty years since my best friend from college, Rick Kleine, insisted it was time for me to write a book. He continued to prod me all these years and it's nice to see that his patience has finally paid off.

I want to say thank you to my cousin, Shelley Prioleau, along with all my wonderful friends and former work colleagues, and to express how meaningful it was whenever you reached out to me. When I was alone in my studio, staring at a blank screen, your kind messages inspired me to start typing.

When I announced to my wife's family that I was taking a hiatus from my career in order to write a book, they offered an immediate and passionate toast to my success. Through the course of my two-year journey, they took a genuine interest in my progress and offered up a Maker's Mark for the completion of every important milestone.

My son, Ryan, also was an enthusiastic supporter from the get go. Cheering me on the whole time, his gift to me upon completion was to hire a professional photographer to take the photo I used on the back cover. What I love most about this gesture is that he wanted to be personally connected to the book. In this and so many other ways, he is.

And finally: As I began work every morning, I glanced at a photo of my brothers and sisters and put out the intention that my book would – in some small but meaningful way – have a healing effect on our family. *"Let my soul smile through my heart and my heart smile through my eyes, that I may scatter rich smiles in sad hearts."* Paramanhansa Yogananda

REFERENCES

Aburdeen, Patricia. *Megatrends 2010*. Charlottesville, VA: Hampton Roads Publishing, 2005.

Alberti, Fay Bound. *The Emotional Heart: Mind, Body and Soul*. New Haven, CT: Yale University Press, 2007

Barks, Coleman. *A Year With Rumi*. San Francisco, CA: Harper Collins, 2006

Becker, Christina. *The Heart of the Matter*. Wilmette, IL: Chiron Publications, 2004

Begley, Sharon. *Train Your Mind. Change Your Brain*. New York: Ballentine Books, 2007

Bracewell, Michael. *The Broken Heart: The Story of the Heartbreak Hotel*. New Haven, CT: Yale University Press, 2007

Childre, Doc. *Heart-Based Living*. Boulder Creek, CA: HeartMath, 2007.

Childre, Doc and Creyer, Bruce. *From Chaos to Coherence: The Power to Change Performance*. Boston, MA. Butterworth-Heinemann, 1999.

Coelho, Paulo. *The Alchemist*. San Francisco: Harper Collins, 1993

Covey, Stephen. *The 7 Habits of Highly Effective People*. New York: Simon and Schuster, 1989.

Dalai Lama. *The Art of Happiness*. New York: Penguin Group, 1998

Dalai Lama. *An Open Heart: Practicing Compassion in Everyday Life*. New York: Little, Brown and Company, 2001.

De Botton, Alain. *The Pleasures and Sorrows of Work*. New York, Random House, 2009.

Emoto, Masaru. *The Hidden Messages in Water*. Hillsboro, OR: Beyond Words Publishing, 2001.

Forbes, Gordon. *Dick Vermiel: Whistle in His Mouth, Heart on His Sleeve*. Chicago, IL: Triumph Books, 2009.

Gelb, Michael. *How To Think Like Leonardo da Vinci*. New York: Random House, 1998.

Goleman, Daniel. *Emotional Intelligence: Why It Can Matter More Than IQ*. New York: Bantam Books, 1995.

Guarneri, Erminia. *The Heart Speaks: A Cardiologist Reveals the Secret Language of Healing*. New York: Simon and Schuster, 2006.

Heath, Chip and Heath, Dan. *Made To Stick: Why Some Ideas Survive and Others Die*. New York: Random House, 2007.

Heider, John. *The Tao of Leadership: Lao Tzu's Tao Te Ching Adopted for a New Age*. New York: Bantam Books, 1985.

Hoystead, Ole. *A History of the Heart*. London: Reaktion Books, 2007

King, Stephen. *On Writing: A Memoir of the Craft*. New York: Scribner, 2000.

Kouses, James and Posner, Barry: *The Leadership Challenge: How to Keep Getting Extraordinary Things Done in Organizations*. San Francisco: Jossey-Bass Publishers, 1995.

LaMott, Anne. *Bird By Bird: Some Instructions on Writing and Life*. New York: Random House, 1994.

Lewis, Michael. *The Big Short: Inside The Doomsday Machine*. New York, W.W. Norton Publishers, 2010.

Maxwell, John. *The 21 Irrefutable Laws of Leadership*. Nashville, TN: Thomas Nelson Publishers, 1998.

Myss, Carolyn. *The Anatomy of Spirit*. New York, Three Rivers Press, 1997.

Nathoo, Ayesha. *The Transplanted Heart: Surgery in the 1960's*. New Haven, CT: Yale University Press, 2007

Palmer, Wendy. *The Intuitive Body: Aikido as a Clairsentient Practice*. Berkeley, CA: North Atlantic Books, 1994.

Pearsall, Paul. *The Heart's Code: Tapping the Wisdom and Power of Our Heart's Energy*. New York: Pocket Books, 1998.

Peto, James. Editor, *The Heart*. New Haven, CT: Yale University Press, 2007

Phillips, Roger. *The Heart and the Circulatory System*. www.accessexcellence.org/AE/AEC/CC/heart_background.php.

Reger, John. *Quotable John Wooden*. Nashville, TN: TowleHouse Publishing, 2002.

Sargent, Emily Jo. *The Sacred Heart: Christian Symbolism*. New Haven, CT: Yale University Press, 2007

Tracy, Brian. *Maximum Achievement*. New York: Simon and Schuster, 1993.

Tulgan, Bruce. *Not Everyone Gets a Trophy: How To Manage Generation Y*. San Francisco: Jossey-Bass Publishers, 2009.

Vance, Michael and Deacon, Dianne. *Think Out of the Box*. Pompton, Plains, NJ: Career Press, 1995.

Young, Louisa. *The Human Heart, an Overview*. New Haven, CT: Yale University Press, 2007

Wellcome Trust, *Hearts and Minds: The Heart in Greek Medicine and Philosophy*. www.wellcome.ac.uk/news/2004/Features/WTX023667.htm

Zukav, Gary. *The Dancing Wu Li Masters, an Overview of the New Physics*. New York: William Morrow, 1979.

Made in the USA
San Bernardino, CA
03 April 2017

47582680R10105